The Nation with the Soul of a Church

A HARPER FORUM BOOK

To
Phil Jordan
Steve Wurster
JoAnn Manfra
Mary Kelley

The Nation with the Soul of a Church

Sidney E. Mead

HARPER & ROW, PUBLISHERS
New York, Evanston
San Francisco, London

Grateful acknowledgment is made to the following for permission to reprint copyrighted material:

ABINGDON PRESS for the essay "The Post-Protestant Concept and America's Two Religions" by Sidney Mead, originally published in *Religion In Life* 33 (Spring, 1964): 191–204, copyright © 1964 by Abingdon Press.

THE CHRISTIAN CENTURY FOUNDATION for the essay "In Quest of America's Religion" by Sidney Mead, originally published in *The Christian Century* 87 (June 17, 1970): 752–56, copyright 1970 by The Christian Century Foundation.

CHURCH HISTORY for the essay "The Nation with the Soul of a Church" by Sidney Mead, originally published in *Church History* 36 (Sept., 1967): 1–22.

FORTRESS PRESS for the essay "The Fact of Pluralism and the Persistence of Sectarianism" by Sidney Mead, originally published in *The Religion of the Republic,* Elwyn A. Smith, editor, copyright 1967 by Fortress Press, Philadelphia.

HOLT, RINEHART AND WINSTON for lines from "Mending Wall" from *The Poetry of Robert Frost* edited by Edward Connery Latham. Copyright 1930, 1939, © 1969 by Holt, Rinehart and Winston, Inc. Copyright © 1958 by Robert Frost. Copyright © 1967 by Leslie Frost Ballantine. Reprinted by permission of Holt, Rinehart and Winston, Publishers.

JOURNAL OF CHURCH AND STATE for "Neither Church nor State: Reflections on James Madison's 'Line of Separation' " by Sidney Mead, originally published in *Journal of Church and State* 10 (Autumn, 1968): 349–363, and is used here by permission.

JOURNAL OF CHURCH AND STATE for "Religion, Constitutional Federalism, Rights, and the Court" by Sidney Mead, originally published in *Journal of Church and State* 14 (Summer, 1972): 191–209, and is used here by permission.

FIRST EDITION

Designed by Janice Stern

Library of Congress Cataloging in Publication data

Mead, Sidney Earl, 1904–
  The nation with the soul of a church.
  Includes bibliographical references and index.
  1. United States—Religion—Addresses, essays, lectures. I. Title.
BR515.M45   200'.973   75-9332
ISBN 0-06-065546-1
ISBN 0-06-065547-X pbk.

---

75 76 77 78 79 10 9 8 7 6 5 4 3 2 1

Contents

Preface

The essays here collected represent the central thrust of my work during the past decade. Every one originated as a lecture, and some of them were delivered several times before being published. I am not able to distinguish between a style for speaking and a style for writing. The reader is an absent hearer. The only good reason I can think of for giving a lecture is that one is concerned to present clearly and persuasively a proposition, the acceptance or rejection of which one deems important. Rhetoric is of the essence.

One motif permeates these essays: that there is, and always has been, an unresolved tension between the theology that legitimates the constitutional structure of the Republic and that generally professed and taught in a majority of the religious denominations of the United States. From my study of "religion in American history," as I have for the sake of clarity preferred to call it, this tension became a *concern* in the Quakers' sense. I have dwelt for a long time with the problems it suggests because I thought them important not only for the future health of the religious and national lives of the Republic, but also for the well-being of the individual who is trying to be both good citizen and good church member. I agree with Adrienne Koch that "it would be a sad task to devote many years of a meager human life to the study of men, minds, actions and achievements that were devoid of the glitter and pull of deep human significance."[1] I deplore the present tendency in the name of scholarly objectivity more and more to separate the academic study of religion from overt involvement in and responsibility for any existing institutionalized species of religion.

As a lecture each essay was structured to stand alone. It is as variations on a common theme that they have an overall unity. Because they originated over a period of years they show some development of ideas and refinement of expression as a result of the helpful critical questions and comments received. In preparation for their appearance together several repetitions of matter and form were edited out. But not all, for repetition is an effective rhetorical device, and often ideas become clearer if seen successively in different contexts.

The scholar-teacher's work should tell a story and/or introduce a thesis. But it should also demonstrate how the author's mind works on his material. The best teacher, Alfred North Whitehead observed, giving a neat twist to Ralph Waldo Emerson's remark, is one who gives the students an exhibition of an ignorant man thinking. Notes exist to give scattered clues to the source material, while the text indicates what the author's mind did with it. Most commonly I use citations, not so much to enlist authorities in defense of ideas I feel to be shaky as to mark the trail I have followed through the chaos of recorded events, and to call attention to authors encountered along the way whose insights and ideas I found congenial and helpful.

The first essay, "In Quest of America's Religion," is a good introduction both to the theme and to the author because, in keeping with the tone of *The Christian Century*'s "How My Mind Has Changed" series, it is autobiographical and broadly inclusive. Along the way I concluded that efforts to understand the American way by forcing it into the ancient categories of "church" and "state" resulted in more confusion than enlightenment, and in the fifth essay I argue for the more applicable imagery of James Madison and a succession of Supreme Court justices. Because I encountered points of view that seemed to exhibit a lack of understanding of the rules of the constitutional game we are playing, the sixth essay is devoted to a simple exposition of the structure. The seventh essay, "Religion of (or and) the Republic" seemed appropriate in that place because of its summary nature. It was composed for a symposium on "Religion and the Republic" at the University of Iowa in April 1973. Its style and tone, set by its being a popular lecture before the hometown people, have been retained.

The fact that the fourth essay, "The 'Nation With the Soul of a Church,'" has been given a prominent place in the book edited by Russell E. Richey and Donald G. Jones,[2] means that I have been thrust willy-nilly into the center of what they call "The Civil Religion Debate." Of course, I greatly appreciate the distinction thus bestowed. But on the other hand, I feel something like the folklore hero who, being newly clothed in a coat of tar and feathers and ridden out of town on a rail, allowed that if it weren't for the honor of being in such distinguished company he would have preferred to walk out, alone. For I fear that with the ever more subtle ramification of the "civil religion"[3] topic in the hands of academic virtuosos the relatively simple points I wish to make are in danger of being lost in the shuffle. I seem to hear "a different drummer."

My point is that there is an unresolved theological issue between "America's two religions" (see the second essay) that contributes to the anxious misery inside our society; and my purpose has been to prod some who are theologically more hip than I am into taking it up at the point in our history where it was laid on the table and largely forgotten.[4]

Back of all my writing lies the intuition, made conscious by reading persons as diverse as Alfred North Whitehead and James Branch Cabell, that mankind is marked by the ability to "see" what is potentially present in the experienced actuality, and out of the seeing to create ideals—"formulated aspirations" that stir "in us to have the creatures of earth and the affairs of earth, not as they are, but 'as they ought to be.' " It is the tension thus created that Whitehead called "the gadfly of civilization," while even the commonly irreverent Cabell concluded that "when we note how visibly it sways all life we perceive that we are talking about God."

The fact that these essays originated as lectures means that I am indebted to several schools and many persons who, by inviting me to speak or to participate in conferences, induced me to pull the ideas together and put them down on paper. Outstanding among the lectureships were Cole Lectures at Vanderbilt in 1966; Lyman Beecher Lectures at Yale Divinity School, 1967; Morse Lectures at Union Theological Seminary in New York, 1967; Rauschenbusch Lectures at Colgate-Rochester Divinity School, 1969; and · Warren Lectures at Harvard, also in 1969.

Unlike most publications of recent years, this one owes no thanks to a grant from a foundation. It was made possible by my professional colleagues and members of the staffs of the History Department and the School of Religion of the University of Iowa who, during the ten years of my tenure there, not only provided the congenial atmosphere that encourages such work, but also the indispensable physical setting and practical helps that make it possible.

Much is due to the constant stimulation of inquisitive students, graduate and undergraduate, who responded critically and intelligently to my teaching, the seedbed of all my writing. In a very special class are the four graduate students who as teaching assistants contributed so much to the effective conduct of my work. It seems natural that this volume should be dedicated to them.

The appearance of the book is immediately attributable to Mary Lou Doyle, who as editorial assistant in the School of Religion, and strictly in the line of her duties, in a very nice way practically bullied me into doing necessary work on the essays while she did a magnificent job of editing them.

And finally, Mildred, on whom continuance of my work absolutely depends, and before whom I stand in awe because of her demonstrated ability to live with me for forty-five years.

SIDNEY E. MEAD
University of Iowa
February 12, 1975

1

In Quest of
America's Religion[1]

Church historians in the seminaries were slow to accept the study of "American church history," as it was called when I began teaching in 1940. In those early days I was frequently told that the only reason students elected to study American church history was that they lacked the scholarly tools to study church history properly so-called—ancient, medieval and reformation. In order to live in my chosen field I had to reject the implication that study of the American experience of Christianity could have nothing of substance to add to our understanding of the nature of Christianity.

Meanwhile secular historians of America's social and intellectual history had begun "The Recovery of American Religious History," to quote the title of a paper by Henry F. May. That recovery, May wrote, "may well be the most important achievement [in American historiography] of the last thirty years."[2] It is in this context that my work is done. And in doing it I have sometimes felt like Don Marquis's worm, which discovered, once the digestive juices of the bird that had swallowed it started working, that it was beginning to see things through the bird's eyes.

I can best explain what that means by citing William Clebsch's distinction between an approach to history analogous to "autobiography" and an approach to history analogous to "biography."[3] The approach of church history as such is analogous to autobiography—the story of "the church" as told from the perspective of an inside, participating believer for whom all that history is his personal history because of his mystical identification with the timeless body of Christ. The approach of "profane" history is analogous to "biography"—the story of religion as told from the perspective of one "outside religion's temple" for whom religion "really is as it really does" in the society. This latter is often designated as a functional approach, as distinguished from the believer's proclamation- or witness-approach.

I have found Clebsch's concepts of biographical and autobiographical history more helpful than H. Richard Niebuhr's distinction between "internal" and "external" history,[4] especially since Niebuhr's essentially positivistic definition of "external" history seems to me to insinuate a true believer's judgment in favor of "internal" history and thus provide for less rigorous minds a potential roosting place for defensive obscurantism. The terms "autobiography" and "biography" are relatively neutral, yet one immediately apprehends the difference between them and recognizes the place and validity of both approaches to the common subject matter. Incidentally, this difference can have, indeed already has had, great influence on ecumenicity, insofar as that is exemplified in real dialogue between Roman Catholic and Protestant scholars. In his *The Ecumenical Revolution*,[5] Robert McAfee Brown cites as a great breakthrough the fact that Catholic and Protestant historians are coming to substantial agreement in their understanding of the place and significance of Luther. This agreement, I would note, is possible only because both ceased to write "autobiographical" histories of "the church" and met on the common ground provided by the "biographical" perspective and approach.

My own approach in interpreting *institutionalized* religion in American history is biographical rather than autobiographical. This, I think, is natural for me. I came from outside "the church" as institutionalized, and although I have found very congenial companionship with some professional churchmen, I now realize that I never felt comfortable and seldom felt completely welcome inside their temples. I have sometimes thought that this feeling may be the penalty of having a sense of humor—of being born, as someone has put it, with the gift of laughter and a sense that the world is mad. Humor and religion may be functional equivalents, and in any one individual they are usually mutually exclusive.

At other times I have thought that what I felt was negative grace: the consciousness of belonging to the hosts of the shadow who in the cosmic scene provide the dark background necessary to enhance the inherently dim glow from the candles of the professional children of light. Thus I conceive of my relation to them as symbiotic; I admit that I could not live without them and I hope that they reciprocate this sentiment.

One of my friends has suggested that my feeling of "outsideness" is rooted in a primarily intellectual interest in religiosity and in a habit of reflective thinking that is threatened by the ambiguities and oversimplifications contingent upon the kind of institutionalization cherished by the true believer. Maybe so. In any case, the last juices of desire to dwell in one of the professional churchmen's temples of religion oozed out of me during my years of theological-school faculty meetings. I am reconciled to living outside that temple wherein it is headline news when, after three years of expensive preparation, a few Southern Baptists manage to talk with a few Jews.[6] Such people remind me of the little boy who "stuck in his thumb and pulled out a plum, and cried, 'What a good boy am I!' " Perhaps this attitude makes me a candidate for the late Bishop Pike's Alumni Association of church institutions.

I agree that self-identity is rooted in a sense of solidarity with the ideas and ideals of a historical community (which I understand to be one of Erik Erikson's points). I agree that man is the creature as well as the creator of his culture. I accept for substance thereof Paul Tillich's dictum:

> Religion as ultimate concern is the meaning-giving substance of culture, and culture is the totality of forms in which the basic concern of religion expresses itself. In abbreviation: religion is the substance of culture, culture is the form of religion. Such a consideration definitely prevents the establishment of a dualism of religion and culture.[7]

It seems to me to follow that study of the history of the religion of one's culture is perhaps the most direct and efficacious route to self-understanding, and that insofar as the historian is immersed in his culture (as I am in mine) his history of the religion of his culture is his "internal" history and his approach will be "autobiographical."

In this context the question becomes, What is the religion of the American culture? Historically, of course, Christianity—the "all-pervading religion of the West"—was the religion of Christendom. But the culture of Christendom is now pluralistic, and that of the United States always has been. This means to me that the form of religion offered by any one of the many sects, or all of them collectively, is but one among many live options offered the citizen in the free market of the institutionalized sacred. Granted these two points, my study of religion in American history, whatever else it may be, becomes a quest to discover and delineate *the* religion of the pluralistic culture in which I have lived and moved and had my being.

"Autobiographical" church historians are apt to go astray by assuming that the religion of the American society must be traditional and historical Christianity as defined by "church-oriented religiosity"; that is, as seen exclusively in its specialized institutional forms in our differentiated society. For my part, I have become convinced that the religion of the American culture—what I have called "the religion of the Republic"—is not the Christianity exhibited in the form of any or all of the denominations in our religiously pluralistic society.

During the past fifteen years, as these essays demonstrate, I have devoted much teaching and several articles and lectures to an attempt to delineate the religion of the Republic and to point out how it differs from the religions of the denominations exemplified in their institutional forms, theological and practical. I have hoped thus to prod competent theologians into seeing the theological issue between the two (or more) religions. But I have found that "temple-ists" or sectarians who cannot distinguish either between "denominational" and "societal" religion or between description and evangelization often confuse my attempt with *advocating* a watered-down "Christianity (or religion) in general."

Meanwhile, by coming to a state university (in 1964) I was confronted for the first time with the necessity of teaching undergraduates. In them one meets a cross-section of our society in all its pluralistic complexity and stubborn actuality, ranging from rampant profanity to hidebound sectarianism. I fell in love with the undergraduates and I am probably somewhat starry-eyed where they are concerned. As one might expect in our pluralistic society, the only safe generalization about them is that satisfactory generalizations about them are impossible. My impression is that in a significant number of them there is, on the one hand, a curiosity about religion and, on the other hand, a widespread alienation from "church-oriented religiosity" in all its forms. The teacher of undergraduates also confronts in them the fact of pluralism in our society, which means that he cannot assume any common religious orientation or common understanding of the terms and concepts traditionally used in discussing matters pertaining to religion. Because these terms and concepts are still the stock-in-trade of almost all seminary education, such education is in danger of becoming a positive barrier to discussing religion with, or presenting the claims of religion to, this generation. The traditional language has become obsolete as an instrument for talking about present religious experience. It must be translated into a modern idiom, and unless this is done, many of the "now" generation will have to decide that institutionalized religion is not for them.

I think the primary purpose of teaching—I would be willing to say of all education—is communication. Therefore the question has become for me: How does one communicate to those of the coming generation an understanding of the place and significance of "religion in American history" and its relevance to them?

One recognizes that, as Henry F. May has said, the language of Christianity is "the language in which most Americans, during most of American history, did their thinking about human nature and destiny."[8] But that language, based on the magnificent richness of the imagery of the Bible, not only is as unfamiliar to most of the younger generation as is the Bible itself; they tend to resist knowledge of it, because they so often associate it with what they view as the hypocritical religiosity of the adult "establishment." Such alienation from the past shatters the sense of historical continuity, and with it the sense of oneself as a historical being. And because self-identity is rooted in a sense of solidarity with the being and ideals of a historical community, such alienation from one's past helps to create an identity vacuum.

As I now see it, the primary task of the historian of religion in America is to help members of the "now" generation to see intellectually and accept emotionally the idea that clues to the nature of their true identity are to be found in the thoughts and actions of the "then" generations that preceded them. Thus, as for all teachers of history, the first step for the teacher of the history of religion in America is to arouse in the student the kind of curiosity about the past that will motivate him to study it. It cannot be assumed that American college students have a "natural" interest in their history. On the contrary, an impressive number are anti-history, because, I suspect, the way history courses are often taught in secondary schools fails to communicate an understanding of the practical value of the study for such comprehension of the present as helps one to face the future. My experience leads me to think that once a student sees the relevance of his history to *his* present, he will, if he is given freedom to do so, explore *his* past with a minimum of guidance and prodding. To arouse such curiosity about the past the teacher must be able to communicate a persuasive theory of how and why the study of one's history is relevant to one's present, and he must exemplify in his attitudes and presentations a passionate interest in the study. For, as every good teacher knows, intellectual passion is contagious.

The second step is to find or develop a definition of "religion" inclusive enough to meet the requirements of our complex pluralistic society. Obviously the definition cannot be "temple-ist" or "sectarian" à la Henry Fielding's Parson Thwackum:

When I mention religion I mean the Christian religion; and not only the Christian religion, but the Protestant religion; and not only the Protestant religion, but the Church of England. And when I mention honour, I mean that mode of Divine grace which is not only consistent with, but dependent upon, this religion; and is consistent with and dependent upon no other.[9]

A Thwackum approach to religion in American history would be autobiographical sectarianism, and the result would be witnessing to one of the many particularistic forms of religion in the pluralistic society; in brief, it would be heteronomous indoctrination. This would satisfy only those who dwelt in Thwackum's temple.

Sectarians, however sophisticated, are quick to use the phrase "religion in general" in a pejorative sense. Yet in pluralistic America, and certainly in my classes of religiously heterogeneous students, "religion" must first mean just that, i.e., religion in general. Recognition of this fact is, I think, forced upon us by the American experience. The sectarian's interpretation of, and negative reaction to, this fact bespeaks his attempt to save his temple, in spite of the scriptural warning respecting the results of such idolatry. One might say that his faith is in his temple and not in his God.

A passage in one of Paul Tillich's books suggested to me a more excellent conclusion to be drawn from the history of the American experience with religious freedom and the fact of pluralism. Tillich wrote:

In the depth of every living religion there is a point at which the religion itself loses its importance, and that to which it points breaks through its particularity, elevating it to spiritual freedom and with it to a vision of the spiritual presence in other expressions of the ultimate meaning of man's existence.[10]

There has been much speculation (some of it tinged with envy) about the reasons for Tillich's great appeal to American students. My hunch is that the thought expressed in the quotation above was received as a clear expression by an authority of high visibility of what many students sensed within themselves as a result of their exposure to American pluralism. It suggested a way of reconciling the two elements I noted above: their curiosity about religion—which one may suppose reflects a spiritual yearning—and the rejection of the sectarian institutional forms of religion their society has offered them.

Of course the "vision of the spiritual presence" in all religions must, if it is to live, be given institutional forms. In this regard I can see little hope in the ecumenical movement and the great councils; for to me they represent only a defensive alliance of those who cling to a dying sectarianism or temple-ism. But I am confident that if human life continues on this planet for a few more years, the "spiritual freedom" Tillich spoke of will receive appropriate institutional expression. And then, it seems to me, we shall have the only religion that can unify the one world created by modern technology, which is potentially the Republic of mankind.[11] The American experience, which has undermined real belief in the ultimacy of all sectarian particularities, has cleared the way for the breakthrough Tillich envisioned.

Without claiming to understand exactly what Tillich meant by those words, I have my opinion of what "that" is to which "every living religion points"; namely, that no man is God. This is what I understand to be the functional meaning of "God" in human experience. Whatever "God" may be, if indeed being is applicable to "God," a concept of the infinite seems to me necessary if we are to state the all-important fact about man: that he is finite. This is the premise of all democratic institutions. It is the essential dogma of the religion of the Republic. I agree with Albert Camus that we shall be saved, if at all, by men who "refuse . . . to be deified," by men who "learn to live and to die, and, in order to be a man, . . . refuse to be a god."[12] Every leader might profit from the example of the emperor who kept beside him one whose sole responsibility was to say over and over again, "Remember, you too are mortal." In the Republic "the people" is the emperor. Churches exist in the Republic to remind this sovereign ruler, "You, too, are mortal; you are not God." Historically, the temple-ist has tended to forget his finiteness and to insist that all must conceive and worship his god in his way, has indeed often been willing to kill those who refused. In the model of the Republic, the civil authority intends that the temple-ists shall curb one another by protecting the right of each continually to tell "the other that he is not God."

2

The Post-Protestant Concept and America's Two Religions[1]

The phrase "post-Protestant" has slipped into common usage to describe the present situation in the United States. This development is to be seen in the context of the current popularity of describing aspects of the present scene as "post" something—post-Christian, post-Constantinian, post-Protestant, postliberal, postmodern, postsectarian, postcommunist, not to mention the almost sacred posts of the biblical scholars. At least a brief flutter of recognition is almost certain to come to anyone who can describe another element of the culture as "post" this or that. "Postmanship" has taken its place beside gamesmanship and oneupmanship. Probably we shall have to wait for minds and pens akin to those of Thorstein Veblen and David Riesman for a profound analysis of the current fascination with the idea that any aspect of the present is best understood in its relationship to something that, like the unfortunate Clementine, is "lost and gone forever." Perhaps it signifies the somber mood of those identity-conscious people who are sure there was a past but who can find little basis for assurance that there will be a future.

In this essay my first concern is to examine the concept of post-Protestant America with its corollary that America was once Protestant, and suggest how, when it is accepted as descriptive of the existing situation, it may obstruct clear understanding of Protestantism's present predicament and of how it got that way. My second concern is to suggest an alternative view; namely, that the bedrock assumptions on which the legal structure of the United States rests never were Protestant in any particularistic sense, and therefore there always has been an unresolved tension between the theology of the Republic and that professed in the denominations. This does not mean that the post-Protestant concept, when carefully defined, is without foundation or merit. But when it conveys the impression that the United States was once Protestant in every respect, it can eclipse the theological issue that ought to be recognized, distort the picture of Protestantism's present situation, and confuse the judgment of what is to be done next.

The view that the present is a post-Protestant era, with its implied premise that the United States was once a Protestant nation, has been applied in the interpretation of the present religious situation by Winthrop S. Hudson,[2] Martin E. Marty,[3] and Will Herberg.[4] A summary of their respective positions will enable us to see the general tenor of the argument as well as several of its implications.

Hudson entitles the third section of his book "Protestantism in Post-Protestant America 1914—." His definition of what he means is clear enough:

> To say that the United States had entered a post-Protestant era is not to deny that much of American culture continued to be informed by a distinctly Protestant ethos, nor is it to contend that Protestantism was no longer a factor shaping American life. It is simply to affirm

that the United States had become a pluralistic society in which Protestantism had ceased to enjoy its old predominance and near monopoly of the religious life of the nation.[5]

In answer to the question of when and how the United States became a pluralistic society, Hudson points to the "new immigration" and to how, following World War I, "Roman Catholicism became an increasingly important factor in the life of the nation, and Protestantism was confronted by the difficult problem of adjusting itself to a status of coexistence with another major religious tradition."[6] Meanwhile, Protestantism had been so identified with the American way of life that it had become a "culture religion" and lost its peculiar identity. The so-called new theology, developed during the years of the late nineteenth and early twentieth centuries, tended to invest "the cultural or social process itself with intrinsic redemptive tendencies" and hence to wash out "any real distinction between the church and the world."[7] This, in turn, "cut the nerve of the evangelistic impulse" in the churches, presumably insofar as it had been an impulse to save men out of the world and to stand in judgment over the culture.

In summary, it would seem that to Hudson "post-Protestant" means two things: (1) the loss in the churches of distinctiveness and identity as *Protestant;* and (2) confrontation with pluralism, specifically with "another major religious tradition," in the society. This situation is definitely pictured as something new: the United States *became* a pluralistic society.

The remedy Hudson finds implied in the "confession of 1935" of Harry Emerson Fosdick, the archliberal of the 1920s and '30s:

> We have been all things to all men long enough. We have adapted and adjusted and accommodated and conceded long enough. We have at times gotten so low down that we talked as though the

highest compliment that could be paid to Almighty God was that a few scientists believed in him. Yet all the time, by right, we had an independent standing-ground and a message of our own in which alone there is hope for mankind.[8]

In brief, Hudson seems to pin his hope for the future of Protestantism on the recovery of particularity, which alone can bring a sense of structured identity to stand in judgment against the prevailing "culture religion." This in turn will require the revival of discipline in the churches. As he had argued in a previous book, "An indispensable prerequisite to the renewal of the churches as a dynamic force in American life is the recovery of discipline. The recovery of discipline, in turn, is dependent upon the recovery of the distinctive note of the Christian faith."[9]

He notes that the outstanding place where "vigor and vitality" as well as discipline and distinctiveness have been preserved is in "third force" Protestantism, that is, among "the miscellaneous threefold grouping of Adventist, Fundamentalist, and Holiness churches," and to some extent among Southern Baptists. Within the mainstream denominations, hope for renewal is vested in a few isolated groups, especially among the Presbyterians and Episcopalians and, perhaps, the Lutherans.[10]

I do not think Hudson makes clear just how the recovery of discipline and distinctiveness in the Protestant churches would enable or even help them to adjust "to a status of coexistence with another major religious tradition." Historically it would seem that disciplined particularity in the several religious groups was precisely what stood in the way of peaceful coexistence and had to be toned down before religious pluralism was possible in a commonwealth.

The post-Protestant concept in Marty's *The New Shape of American Religion* is somewhat tangential to the main argument of the book, and in subsequent publications he has greatly qualified his use of it. But in *The New Shape* he held that it is "strict historical accuracy to call these post-Protestant times."[11] At least, he added, "one could certainly not describe these as post-Catholic, post-Jewish, or post-secular times"—which may be true enough, granted one feels compelled to describe them as "post" something. Even so, it might well be argued that if America was once Protestant, it must have been post-Catholic, and post-Jewish.

Like Hudson, Marty begins with the premise that "America was once largely Protestant."[12] By this he means that "insofar as organized religion was represented in the great central events that shaped America and have become part of its mystic core, Protestantism dominated."[13] But today, he continues, we see "the maturing of several processes"—"the erosion of particularity . . . by a blurry, generalizing religion"; the "smoothing of the edges of witness" by an "amiable syncretism"; and the "loss of religious content." This "process of erosion" in Protestantism "has been long and gradual."[14]

What happened in the decade of the 1950s was not a revival of religion but "a revival of *interest* in religion,"[15] and what came to prevail was "religion-in-general." Marty equates this "religion-in-general" with the "national religion." The revival of the 1950s, then, was "the first great awakening not of mainstream Protestant Christianity as such but *of a maturing national religion.*"[16] This was *"The New American Religion,"*[17] and "no term better describes America's new religious constellation than . . . 'religion-in-general.' "[18] It is to be noted that Marty stresses that this "American Religion" is something *new.*

While Herberg does not use the phrase "post-Protestant," a chief concern of his article is to explain "the transformation of America from a *Protestant* country into a *three-religion* country."[19]

He recognizes that because Americans are all immigrants in origin, American society has always been fluid and pluralistic. How then, he asks, does an individual gain and define his peculiar identity and sense of belonging in such a mobile and pluralistic society? His answer is that the United States was once Protestant in the sense that the only acceptable way to be 100 percent American was to be Protestant—something that Americans of other religious groups recognized. America was a one-religion country, and that religion was Protestantism. Today this situation has changed. A "three-religion America has emerged"—Protestant, Catholic, and Jew— "these are three alternative ways of being an American."[20]

In this context Herberg develops his view of the washout of religious particularity. For if religion serves the function of identifying oneself as "American," this function may be "largely unrelated to the content of faith." "Indeed for such a purpose, the *authentic content of faith* may even prove a serious handicap, for . . . it carries a prophetic impact which serves rather to unadjust than to adjust, to emphasize the ambiguity of every earthly form of belonging rather than to let the individual rest secure in his 'sociability.' "[21] This would seem to suggest that *"the authentic content of faith"* is incompatible with willing acceptance of religious pluralism in the society; and, conversely, that if an individual seems to rest secure with such pluralism, this is reason for doubting the authenticity of his faith.

Herberg's argument continues that, having lost their exclusiveness and particularity, the three traditional faiths lend themselves to a vaguer faith that seems to include them all. Americans

are coming to regard . . . the "three great faiths," as three alternative (though not necessarily equal) expressions of a great overarching commitment which they all share by virtue of being Americans. This commitment is, of course, to democracy or the American Way of Life. It is the common allegiance which . . . provides Americans with the "common set of ideas, rituals, and symbols" through which an "overarching sense of unity" is achieved amidst diversity and conflict. It is, in a sense far more real than John Dewey ever dreamed of, the "common religion" of Americans.[22]

After reading that paragraph one expects Herberg to speak next of the theological issues between the "three great faiths" on the one hand and "the 'common religion' of Americans" on the other. Instead, by unequivocally identifying "Americanization" with "secularization"—the process is "essentially the 'Americanization' of religion in America, and therefore its thorough-going secularization"[23]—he seems in effect to deny that the "common religion" is a religion at all and to sidestep the possibility that there is a theological issue between them to be discussed.[24] Often the American's "ultimate commitment" is to "the American Way of Life," which is secular. But, Herberg continues, the American "combines the two—his [Jewish-Christian?] religion and his culture [the common religion?]—by making the former an expression of the latter, his religion an expression of the 'moral and spiritual values of democracy.' "[25] Herberg's conclusion is that "we have in America an invisible, formally unacknowledged, but very potent religion—the religion of democracy, the religion of the American Way of Life—of which the conventional religions are felt to be more or less adequate expressions."[26] Thus Herberg does appear to give more tangible content to Hudson's concept of "culture religion" and Marty's concept of "religion-in-general." But he does not seem to notice that what he has described with fair accuracy is the religious stance of the founding fathers, and it is hard to understand why he insists that the "religion of democracy" is invisible and formally unacknowledged—a point to which we shall return.

In summary, the concept of post-Protestant America as delineated by these men contains the following premises: that the United States was once Protestant; that it is no longer so; that Protestantism, Catholicism, and Judaism because, or as, they lost their particularity and relinquished discipline were overshadowed by the religion of democracy (or culture religion, or religion-in-general, or "the civic religion") which concurrently emerged. At least to Herberg the religion of democracy is thoroughgoing secularism. All three employ this complex concept to interpret the present religious situation in the United States. And they come to essentially the same conclusion regarding the nature of Protestantism's present sickness; namely, it is a loss of particularity, a religious anemia, so to speak. Hence they point to essentially the same remedy: the recovery of particularity and discipline in the churches.

This entire view rests primarily on the first premise, that the United States was once a Protestant nation. No doubt this is sound enough if one means only that the Protestant churches apparently exerted more influence in shaping the mores than did other religious groups. But it is patently false when applied to what may be called the theology of the Republic, upon which rests the thinking behind the Declaration of Independence, the Constitution, and the long line of court decisions on matters pertaining to religious freedom. Henry Steele Commager seems to me to have had the right distinction in mind when he wrote that "in everything but law, America, at the opening of the 20th century, was a Christian nation."[27] The exception "in everything but law" is very important, for the legal structure is the skeleton that holds up the meat of the body politic. The United States was never Protestant in the sense that its constitutional and legal structure was rooted in or legitimated by particularistic Protestant theology. To overlook this is to confuse or completely to bypass unresolved theological issues between the denominations and the civil authority. The issue is between the theology of the Republic's legal structure, which defines even the nature and limits of religious freedom, and the theology of the denominations, which defines their self-identity and correlative reasons for separate existence. The question is, Are the two theologies reconcilable; and if so, how; and if not, which is to be chosen?

This question is not of recent origin but began to take shape at the beginning of colonization. The problem has not arisen because the United States was once Protestant, or even Christian in a particularistic sense, and has *become* pluralistic. Hudson, I think, is wrong in supposing that only in the twentieth century was Protestantism "confronted by the difficult problem of adjusting itself to a status of coexistence with another major religious tradition." As Marty notes, "America knew a nascent pluralism from the time two men of different faiths set foot on its shore with intention to remain."[28] The question was built into the structure of the United States with the Constitution, for obviously the theological assumptions underlying its provisions for religious freedom could not be distinctively Protestant or even Christian.[29] Therefore, while the recovery of Protestant particularity and discipline in the churches is important enough for other reasons, it would not necessarily help to resolve the tension between America's two religions—and might indeed accentuate it. A great deal would depend, for example, on whose particularity was recovered from the pluralistic grab bag—whether that of John Cotton or of Roger

Williams, of Isaac Backus or of Timothy Dwight, of C. F. W. Walther or of Samuel S. Schmucker, of Reinhold Niebuhr or of Carl McIntyre.[30]

G. K. Chesterton, somewhat irked and then amused by the questions he was asked when he applied for a passport to the United States, was led to ask what it is that "makes America peculiar."[31] He concluded that it was the fact that

> America is the only nation in the world that is founded on a creed. That creed is set forth with dogmatic and even theological lucidity in the Declaration of Independence. . . . It enunciates that all men are equal in their claim to justice, and that governments exist to give them that justice, and that their authority is for that reason just. It certainly does condemn anarchism, and it does also by inference condemn atheism, since it clearly names the Creator as the ultimate authority from whom these equal rights are derived.[32]

The crucial question for those who use the post-Protestant concept is, What is the theology of this American creed? Assuredly it is not Protestant in any particularistic sense. Leading Protestants around the close of the eighteenth century dubbed it "infidelity," the precise meaning of which was the denial of a special revelation in the Bible; and men like Timothy Dwight of Connecticut went to great lengths to prove that from a Christian point of view it was "vain and deceitful"—a slippery path to eternal damnation.[33] It was rationalism, or deism, or natural religion—names descriptive of the perspective of most of the men who had a hand in framing the Declaration and the Constitution and in launching the new government. It is for this reason that Marty can say:

> The spokesmen of the "Religion of Democracy" school [today] are . . . appropriating an authentic parcel of the American past. They

are more accurate in their reading of the founding fathers than are the unthinking Christians who try to make Protestants out of them and who try to theologize all the basic documents of our national history on Christian lines.[34]

On the other hand, those who try to make secularists—in the classical sense[35]—out of them are just as wrong.

It was this theology that made theoretically acceptable the scandal of Christendom at the time—acceptance by a nation of religious pluralism and the consequent multiplicity of independent religious groups. One might say that the provisions in the Constitution and First Amendment for national religious freedom and separation of church and state were conceived in actual religious pluralism and were dedicated to the proposition that all religions are equal. They are, as Jefferson said, "of various kinds, indeed, but all good enough; [because] all sufficient to preserve peace and order." This it is that is scandalous to all Christian particularity.

The theology back of this view, and the religious stance of those who held it, is delightfully delineated by Benjamin Franklin in his *Autobiography*:

I had been religiously educated as a Presbyterian; and tho' some of the dogmas of that persuasion, such as the *eternal decrees of God, election, reprobation, etc.*, appeared to me unintelligible, others doubtful, and I early absented myself from the public assemblies of the sect, Sunday being my studying day, I never was without some religious principles. I never doubted, for instance, the existence of the Deity; that he made the world, and govern'd it by his Providence; that the most acceptable service of God was the doing of good to man; that our souls are immortal; and that all crime will be punished, and virtues rewarded, either here or hereafter. These I esteem'd the essentials of every religion; and, being to be found in all the religions we had in our country, I respected them all, tho' with different degrees of respect, as I found them more or less mix'd with other articles, which, without any tendency to inspire, promote, or confirm morality, serv'd principally to divide us, and make us unfriendly to one another. This respect to all, with an opinion that the worst had some good effects, induc'd me to avoid all discourse that might tend to lessen the good opinion another might have of his own religion; and as . . . new places of worship were continually wanted, and generally erected by voluntary contribution, my mite for such purpose, whatever might be the sect, was never refused.[36]

Recognition that this outlook was widely prevalent among the founding fathers is enough to undermine the supposition that "religion-in-general," or the "religion of democracy . . . of which the conventional religions are felt to be more or less adequate expressions," emerged only in the twentieth century. This theology is not only *not* particularistic; it is designedly antiparticularistic, in this respect reflecting the predominant intellectual slant of the eighteenth century. These thinkers held that only what is common to all religions and all sects—Franklin's "essentials of every religion"—is relevant to the being and well-being of the *common*-wealth. This is the theology behind the legal structure of America, the theology on which the practice of religious freedom is based and its meaning interpreted. Under it, one might say, it is religious particularity, Protestant or otherwise, that is heretical and schismatic—even un-American!

When the churches accepted religious freedom on these terms, they put themselves into a bind. For under such freedom each group was thrown into competition with all the others, and in this situation must base its claim for allegiance and support on its distinctiveness. At the same time, to become "American" has always meant, implicitly at least, to accept the theology of America's creed and to renounce traditional particularity along with the devil of sectarianism and all his works. The issue with which religious freedom confronted the churches was an issue between two religions—theirs and that of the Declaration.

Nor has the religion of democracy been "invisible [and] formally unacknowledged," as apparently Herberg would have it. It has been celebrated on its holy days, notably the Fourth of July, Memorial and Thanksgiving days, in proclamations and in speeches. One has but to visit a service club to see with what seriousness its cult practices are observed and its hymn sung; or to visit the Lincoln Memorial in Washington to see with what devotion its shrines are visited and attended.[37] Recently it has developed its ardent particularists—its fundamentalist sects—in the so-called far, or radical, or reactionary "right."

Church members in America have always been faced with the necessity to choose, implicitly at least, between the inclusive religion of democracy and the particularistic Christianity of their sect. Few have been as articulate about this as Thomas Sugrue, a New England Roman Catholic of Irish descent.[38] His church, he complained, did "not introduce him to God, or to the deep gregariousness of the spiritual life," but rather, acquainted him "with religious sectarianism, and with the dismal fact that in his relation to God he must through all his life be separated from the majority of his fellow men, whom God has informed him are his brothers, and commanded him to love."[39] Confronted with the conflict of religions, he chose the religion of democracy:

All religious roads lead in the end to God, just as all rivers eventually, reach the sea; pilgrims on these highways know that this is so, and realize that many roads are necessary for the many kinds of people, who begin their spiritual journeys from a multitude of points of view. It is the commanders of the highways who will not have it so; each wants preferential rating for his thoroughfare, and longs to reduce all other turnpikes to the status of tributary.[40]

Similar was the conclusion of the Congregationalist Josiah Strong, who, in his very popular book *Our Country,* first published in 1885, also echoed Benjamin Franklin's sentiments:

The teaching of the three great fundamental doctrines which are common to all monotheistic religions is essential to the perpetuity of free institutions, while the inculcation of sectarian dogmas is not. These three doctrines are that of *the existence of God, the immortality of man,* and *man's accountability.* These doctrines are held in common by all Protestants, Catholics, and Jews.[41]

Strong and Sugrue found the particularistic theology of their sects in conflict with the inclusive theology of the Republic in which they lived, and, in effect, they chose the latter. And I suspect there are many clergymen and lay people in the churches in America who occupy a similar position without being aware of the theological gulf they are straddling. They participate in the activities of their churches, including all the observances, but their real theology is that of the Republic. It was this phenomenon that intrigued Herberg. He seems to me correctly to have noted that America "has its underlying culture-religion . . . of which the three conventional religions [Protestant, Catholic, Jew] are somehow felt to be appropriate manifestations and expressions. Religion is integral to Americanism as currently understood."[42] My only question about this view is the implication that the condition noted is something new. It seems to me a fair description of the position of the founding fathers as exemplified in the foregoing quotation from Franklin.

In this context the prevalence of Hudson's "culture religion,"

Marty's "religion-in-general," and Herberg's "civic religion" is seen not as a new emergent, but as the popular triumph of the theology of the Declaration over the theology of the competing denominations. Marty noted this but did not develop its import when he quoted Oscar Handlin: "The Enlightenment prevailed over 'the forms American religion took in its development from Calvinism.' "[43] So Marty saw that during the period of growth and expansion

> while Protestants pointed with pride to their achievements they hardly realized that the typically rationalist view of the irrelevancy of theological distinction in a pluralist society was pulling the rug out from under them. For a long time a Protestant majority gloried in its bluff, not noticing the winds which were eroding its position and its distinctiveness.[44]

Seen in this perspective the statements of the late Dwight David Eisenhower, which have often been cited to illustrate the *new* American religious stance, take on quite a different significance. In 1948 the general said, "I am the most intensely religious man I know. Nobody goes through six years of war without a faith. That does not mean that I adhere to any sect." In 1952, shortly after his election, the president said, "Our government makes no sense unless it is founded in a deeply felt religious faith, and I don't care what it is." In 1955 he declared that "recognition of the Supreme Being is the first, the most basic expression of Americanism. Without God, there could be no American form of government, nor an American way of life." Eisenhower's position in this respect, far from being "new," seems directly in the tradition of the founding fathers. Indeed, a century before their day, in 1675, the then Lord Baltimore spoke with approval of Maryland's toleration for "all sorts who professed Christianity in general." Thus early he seems to have suggested the question whether the traditional religious particularity was compatible with religious toleration—a question Protestants have not unequivocally answered. Benjamin Franklin stopped going to hear the minister whose sermons seemed designed "rather to make us Presbyterians than good citizens"—suggesting no minister could do both.

Our common concern is for the future. And, as Chesterton said, "We can be almost certain of being wrong about the future, if we are wrong about the past." If one begins with a concept of the present situation as "post-Protestant," it is natural to make the suppositional deduction that the United States was once wholly Protestant. This in turn stands in the way of seeing the true nature of the theological substratum of the Declaration, the Constitution, and the court decisions. Hence "religion-in-general" appears to signify a *new* attitude toward religion, or to be a "new national religion" rather than the popular triumph of the old inclusive theology of the Republic over the particularistic theology of the denominations. Ignoring the tension between the two religions which has existed from the beginning enables one to diagnose Protestantism's present anemia as due primarily to the loss of particularity and discipline and to prescribe their recovery as the remedy. Slighting the Creator-centered theology of the American creed (in Chesterton's sense) enables one to identify Americanization with "thoroughgoing secularization" to which, it is implied, Protestant, Catholic, and Jew in order to be true to the authentic content of their faiths must be opposed.

But not only does entertainment of the concept tend to back one into this box, it tends also to confuse the issues of the present in a way reminiscent of the battle with "infidelity" during the late eighteenth and early nineteenth centuries. No doubt secularization in the classical sense of practical atheism is a common enemy before which the lines between the three faiths—Protestant, Catholic, Jewish—fade into relative insignificance. But, I would add, so do the lines between them and the religion of the Republic. This is what men like Timothy Dwight did not recognize in their day, so they spurned the potential help of such "infidels" as Thomas Paine, who directed his *Age of Reason* and later writings against the common enemy, atheism. Marty has suggested that in doing so they "were fighting what amounted to 'the wrong war at the wrong place, at the wrong time and with the wrong enemy.'" And insofar as we permit "secularism" to become an "all-purpose concept" similar to what "infidelity" became in Dwight's time, we court the tragic irony of re-enacting the entire struggle "in our time in relation to this newer catch-all term."[45]

On the other hand, recognition that the theology undergirding the practice of religious freedom has always been in conflict with the distinctive theology of right-wing Protestantism enables one to diagnose Protestantism's present sickness as a psychosomatic indigestion, resulting from an inability either to digest the theology on which the practice of religious freedom rests or to regurgitate the practice. I am told that an animal that cannot regurgitate can be killed by getting it to accept as food something it cannot digest. I do not think Protestantism can give up the practice of religious freedom which it has accepted. Therefore, I conclude, if it cannot learn to digest the theory on which such freedom rests, the prognosis cannot be a happy one.

There is a largely neglected strand in the Protestant tradition representing the attempt to come to terms theologically with religious pluralism and, indeed, to see it as a positive good. Winthrop Hudson delineated its emergence among some of the Independent divines of seventeenth-century England.[46] From thence I think it might be traced historically through eighteenth-century pietistic and evangelical movements to its flowering in the formation of the Evangelical Alliance in 1846. By that time its leaders had adumbrated a doctrine of the church (denominationalism as over against sectarianism) consistent with the practice of religious freedom. But, for whatever reasons, their work has become an almost forgotten chapter in American church history. Perhaps one reason is that any group would have to risk losing its life of particularistic distinctiveness in order to move in the direction suggested by the evangelicals.[47] How very difficult this possibility is to entertain is illustrated by the stance assumed by those who hold the post-Protestant concept we have been examining. Perhaps if leading churchmen were more willing to risk the loss of their understanding and practice of the faith—of its particularity—instead of clinging to its denominational swaddling clothes of distinctiveness, there would be more hope for a renewal of life.

Possibly there is merit in what appears just now to be a very minor refrain:

> What we are beginning to realize is that God in his providence has permitted a common type of faith and life to emerge from the freedom and the denominational variegation of American Christianity. Out of separate historical traditions which find it increasingly difficult to maintain their relevance we find ourselves meeting one another with common convictions, a common sense of mission, and common methods of doing our work. Many of us would like to join in a large-scale union.[48]

3

The Fact of Pluralism and the Persistence of Sectarianism[1]

Any attempt to understand the religious situation in America must begin with recognition of the fact of pluralism. Philip Schaff, seeing this fact in historical perspective, declared in 1855 that the United States presented "a motley sampler of all church history, and the results it has thus far attained."[2] During the century since Schaff wrote, the pluralism has been augmented until, as Mr. Justice Brennan noted in the Murray-Schempp decision, religiously we are

> a vastly more diverse people than were our forefathers. They knew differences chiefly among Protestant sects. Today the Nation is far more heterogeneous religiously, including as it does substantial minorities not only of Catholics and Jews but as well of those who worship according to no version of the Bible and those who worship no God at all.[3]

In this essay I have attempted, first, to analyze some of the implications of this basic fact and, second, to note the persistence of "sectarian" reactions to it.

Traditionally in Christendom, and clearly after the Reformation and the emergence of nations, it was almost universally assumed that the being and continued well-being of a civil commonwealth depended upon there being religious uniformity within it. The church was the institution that defined, articulated, and inculcated the common religious beliefs and developed the forms of ecclesiastical structure, discipline, and worship deemed necessary. It was the guardian of the nation's tribal cult. Church and state were separate only in the sense that they had different functions in promoting the common end of both, which was the glory of God. The first charter and early laws for Virginia make this clear. They assert that the king's "principall care" in all his realms is "true religion, and reuerence to God." In keeping with this view, the laws were "declared against what Crimes soeuer, whether against the diuine Majesty of God, or our soueraigne, and Liege Lord, King James."

Here the established church was not abstract and invisible, but an institutionalized authority alongside the civil authority. Together they represented the dual power structure of the *common*-wealth. Clergy and magistrates represented two distinct but related authorities in the body politic, and most of the problems of church and state rose out of conflicts between them.

In this context the question of the relationship between church and state, while often puzzling, is at least definable because one is talking about the relation between two institutions, each represented by officials. As the state was the persons vested with the authority of civil government, so the church was the persons vested with the authority of ecclesiastical government.

This situation existed for so long in Christendom that there came to be practically universal intellectual acceptance and justification of such "Establishment."

With the emergence of a commonwealth with religious pluralism during the seventeenth and eighteenth centuries, something new appeared—or perhaps something as old as the pre-Constantinian Roman Empire reappeared. In any case it appeared to be so new in America that the founders defended it primarily as an experiment worth trying. The American experiment was to find out whether a commonwealth could exist and flourish "with a full liberty in religious concernments" and a plurality of religious groups, each claiming in traditional fashion exclusively to be "the church."

Such religious diversity had become an accepted fact of the experienced order of things without the intention of the nation's civil-ecclesiastical authorities. As Reinhold Niebuhr has put it:

> Most of the proponents of the various religious positions did not really believe in either freedom or toleration. Freedom came to the Western world by the providence of God and the inadvertance of history. Tolerance was an absolute necessity for a community which had lost its religio-cultural unity and could find peace only if toleration and freedom were accepted.[4]

By and large, in America civil authority forced toleration upon reluctant churchmen, most of whom finally saw that the only way they could get freedom for themselves was to grant it to all others.

But it is one thing for a religious group of necessity to accept and adapt outwardly to a radical change in the experienced order of events, and quite another thing to reformulate and accept the change in the conceptual order necessary to make it compatible with the changed experienced order thrust upon it by what Alfred North Whitehead called the force of "senseless agencies." My suggestion is that as religious freedom became an inescapable fact of the experienced order—its newness evidenced by a multiplicity of religious groups in a commonwealth—churchmen and theologians were called upon to develop new concepts to enable new ways of explaining and defending what they accepted in practice.

We think by relating concepts. We experience concrete details, but we must think in abstract generalizations. My suggestion implies that the traditional concepts of Christendom ("church" and "state") used to think about the relationship between civil government and religious institutions are not applicable, and likely to be confusing, in attempting to think about the new situation created by the kind of religious freedom actualized in the American experiment.

In the United States "the church," in the sense that the words conveyed in Christendom for centuries, simply does not exist. "The church" is not an aspect of the American's experienced order. Rather, it exists as an abstract concept, a figure of speech, a theological assertion, pointing beyond the actual and confusing diversity of sects to the pious faith that each is a part of the unbroken body of Christ. For this reason alone the old concepts of church and state no longer describe the actuality experienced. The church as such is not a recognized legal entity in the United States at all.[5] This is what the American observes and experiences.

What one sees and how he conceives it are of course inseparable. The unit is an observation. Details experienced are "invariably interpreted in terms of the concepts supplied by the conceptual order" which Whitehead describes as "a rough system of ideas in terms of which we do in fact interpret" our experiences.[6] In this context, novel observations ought sooner or later to be reflected in modifications of the conceptual order. But, and especially if, the conceptual order of the observer has an aura of sacredness about it rooted in his unreflective acceptance of his religious tradition, he may cling to it, stubbornly thinking he ought to try to make the new experienced order again conform to it.[7]

This, I think, is the point at which theologians often find themselves at odds with Supreme Court justices. Theologians, in discussing the relation between civil authority and their religion, commonly attempt to make the profane civil matters conform to their sacred conceptual order. For example, the court's attempt to maintain the necessary religious neutrality of the civil authority is interpreted as a thrust toward the establishment of a "secular religion."[8]

We all face a very complex situation. A multiplicity of religious groups implies a great diversity of religious beliefs, each given more or less systematic intellectual structure in theological systems. And because a religious commitment is an all-or-nothing matter for the one who holds it, the builder of a theological system, whether amateur or professional, aspires to delineate a complete conceptual order. Pluralism means that two people may bring quite different conceptual orders to an event both experience. In this sense they live in different worlds, and they simply do not, and cannot, "see" the same thing in it. Therefore, while everyone in the commonwealth may apparently share a commonly experienced order of events, the things seen do not have the same meaning for them. Consequently different people react quite differently to the same event, as witness the emotion-laden reactions to the school Bible reading and prayer decisions, or to the abolition of the Blaine Amendment in New York.

The confusion thus created is compounded because key words and phrases may mean quite different things in the context of different conceptual orders. Two persons may use the same words and phrases and each may think the other is talking about the same thing he is, when actually their minds are not meeting at all. Obvious examples are the words *church, state, establishment, free exercise,* and, most confusing of all, *separation.* All the key words used in the discussion of the relation between civil authority and religion are for this reason ambiguous. Even the word *God* had become so ambiguous long before theologians announced his death that the Federal Communications Commission was led to declare in July 1946 that "so diverse are these conceptions that it may be fairly said, even as to professed believers, that the God of one man does not exist for another."[9] This is one of the most obvious results of our basic freedoms and religious pluralism.

But the United States *is* a *common*wealth. We are all, as Thomas Jefferson held and James Baldwin says he discovered in Paris, "American."[10] To think about this sense of common identity as Americans one must, I believe, entertain some such concept as philosopher Alfred North Whitehead called "a general form of the forms of thought"[11] of an age and place; what anthropologist Ruth Benedict refers to as the constellation of "ideas and standards" that define a culture and bind its people together;[12] what economist Adolf A. Berle, Jr., defines as the "public consensus";[13] and what historian Ralph Gabriel calls "social ideas."[14] These "ideas and standards" or the "general form" are of such high generality that they "rarely receive any accurate verbal expression." They are, as Whitehead put it, "hinted at through their special forms appropriate to the age in question," in a cross, a flag, a star, through poetry, the arts, and rituals. For example, the flag is the symbol of the unity of America and what it stands for.[15]

Therefore, although the "ideas and standards" lie at the heart of a culture, usually they are but faintly impressed upon the conscious rational minds of the people in that culture. Yet within a culture the great conversation that makes a civilization possible can go on only because and so long as a significant number of the participants share these high generalities which provide the premises of the dialogue.

However, the participants in the heat of a discussion of controverted issues, speaking as each does out of his own set of specific notions, easily lose sight of the high generalities they share with all the others. Anyone who has lived in an academic community will immediately recognize the phenomenon to which Whitehead refers:

> It is difficult even for acute thinkers to understand the analogies between ideas expressed in diverse phraseologies and illustrated by different sorts of examples. Desperate intellectual battles have been fought by philosophers [and theologians] who have expressed the same idea in different ways.[16]

A striking example of such a battle is provided by the conflict between defenders of New England orthodoxy and the "infidels" during the late eighteenth and early nineteenth centuries. Although they never actually crossed swords, we may take Lyman Beecher of Connecticut and Thomas Jefferson as representatives of the respective parties. The prime premise of Jefferson's "Act for Establishing Religious Freedom in Virginia" was that the use of coercion in matters of religious belief was "a departure from the plan of the Holy Author of our religion, who being Lord both of body and mind, yet chose not to propagate it by coercions on either, as was in his Almighty power to do." The basic premise of Lyman Beecher's theological model was that "when God has formed moral beings, even he can govern them, as such, only by moral influence, and in accordance with the laws of mind: mere omnipotence being as irrelevant to the government of mind, as moral influence would be to the government of the material universe."[17]

Beecher and Jefferson, although bitter antagonists on the level of "specific notions," seem to me to have been in agreement on the high generality that the essential nature of Deity in his relationships with men is persuasion and not coercion—the intuition respecting "the nature of things" that Christianity meant to incarnate in actual practice.

Eventually Beecher came to the same conclusion as did Jefferson respecting religious freedom in a commonwealth—a deduction from the common principle. But for many years, until after disestablishment in Connecticut in 1818, contrary to that principle he defended the standing order, which meant coerced tax support for his type of the public worship of God. Meanwhile Jefferson in his First Inaugural Address had noted that "every difference of opinion is not a difference of principle," and that in the political controversies "we have called by different names brethren of the same principle. We are all Republicans, we are all Federalists"; that is, we are all Americans. Forty years later some Protestant evangelical churchmen were proclaiming what to them was their "new" idea that although Protestants were divided into many competing organizations they were all "Christians." And only recently did a significant number of Protestants and Catholics begin to refer to each other as brethren of their common Christian faith.

I agree with what appears to have been the conclusions reached by Anson Phelps Stokes in his massive three-volume study of *Church and State in the United States*—that the high generality on which religious liberty rests is now an ineradicable part of that constellation of ideas and standards that defines the world-view behind the American way of life. But for centuries, although latently ever present in the universality inherent in the Christian tradition, it was certainly not a prominent element among the specific notions that defined the sects and nations of Christendom. It did not, in Herbert Butterfield's words, get into the "majority report" of Christians.

The mainline denominations of the United States, the direct descendants of the national churches of Europe, had been formed in the old national-church crucible, and each elaborated the rationale for its sense of identity and its justification for separate existence in that context. That these national tribal cults were transplanted to what was to become the United States meant that here Christianity—"the all-embracing culture religion of the West"[18]—was poured into "sectarian" molds and hardened in those distinct but now crumbling shapes which we see in our denominations.

Because religious commitment is an all-or-nothing matter, each religious group tended to absolutize the particular tenets of its generally Christian theology and polity that distinguished it from all others. For in these its sense of peculiar and significant identity and its justification for separate existence were rooted. As L. W. Bacon noted in his *History of American Christianity,* published in 1895:

> The presumption is of course implied, if not asserted, in the existence of any Christian sect, that it is holding the absolute right and truth, or at least more nearly that than other sects; and the inference, to a religious mind, is that the right and true must, in the long run, prevail.[19]

It is for this reason that every religious group tends to resist emphasis on the tenets it shares with all others; to resist, for example, consistent probing for the high generalities implied in such phrases as "a common core of religion," "Christianity in general," or "religion in general," or the eighteenth century's "the essentials of every religion." Because theology in the grand tradition has to do with the high generalities of Christianity and its culture, this built-in aversion to inclusive or cosmopolitan abstractions helps to explain the often-noted untheological nature of American religious groups.[20]

This innate tendency was accentuated in the United States because religious freedom put each group (now a voluntary association) in a competitive relationship with all the others, not only for the allegiance of the uncommitted in the great free market of souls, but also for those committed to other groups. Christians developed extensive programs for the conversion of Jews; Protestants maintained havens for "converted" priests; Roman Catholics publicized the conversion of prominent people from Orestes Brownson to Luci Johnson; fundamentalists tried to win liberals; liberals tried to enlighten fundamentalists; while the Unitarians almost automatically welcomed any refugee from the disciplinary action of another denomination.

Competitors, whether "selling" cigarettes or religion, are seldom inclined to stress the virtues of their competitors' claims and practices, or to dwell upon the good and valuable elements they share in common with them. Yet in the religiously pluralistic commonwealth inclusive generalities are the only viable concepts of general application.

Pluralism means, then, not only the division into many different ecclesiastical organizations and theological points of view, but also a state of mind instinctively defensive of it. The resulting confusion was described by Professor Wilhelm Pauck in 1963:

> The denominations [in the United States] preserve and cling to special religious traditions, creeds (if they have any), liturgies, polities, moral codes, in a stubborn and even self-satisfied way, as if no other forms of Christian faith or order existed or have the right to exist. Think, for example, of the behavior of some Lutherans, Unitarians, Presbyterians, or Episcopalians, to mention only these, who

stick to their own particular traditions with a dogged determination. . . . But . . . they grant to members of other denominations the right to hold and practice the same judgment concerning their beliefs, usages and conventions. Denominationalism is thus a curious combination of tolerance and intolerance. On the one hand, it reflects the exclusiveness that was the characteristic of the churches when in the era prior to the establishment of religious freedom they had to conform to the requirements of religious uniformity. On the other hand, it exhibits the freedom of religious profession which was made possible when the modern state assumed a neutral attitude toward the religious faith of its members and citizens.[21]

This situation, only slightly changed by the ecumenical movement, exhibits not only the intellectual confusion, but also the continuing tension between the many particularistic and inherited conceptual orders of the sects of Christendom and that new experienced order that came with religious freedom and religious pluralism in a commonwealth. I take it that concern about this situation and an urge to do something about it provide a strong motivation for ecumenical endeavors.

But the fact that the commonwealth exists implies that at its center must lie a constellation of ideas and standards that bind its people together—what Abraham Lincoln in his First Inaugural Address referred to as the "bonds of affection; the mystic chords of memory" that constitute the score for "the chorus of the Union." And it seems to me that the "bonds of affection" which bind all the heterogeneous people together in such a union must somehow be more cosmopolitan, more universal, more general, than the "bonds of affection" which bind a particular group of these people together in a particular voluntary association, even though it be called a church. Will Herberg should not have been surprised to discover that the girls in that Catholic school thought of themselves as "Americans who happen to be Roman Catholics."[22] For being an American today is for most citizens a matter of providence or a happenstance of birth rooted in a choice made by an immigrant ancestor, while being a Catholic, a Presbyterian, a Baptist, an Episcopalian, or a Lutheran is a matter of voluntary choice.

Finally, then, religious pluralism means that the issue commonly referred to as being between church and state is for the church member an issue between his outlook as a citizen and his outlook as a member of a religious denomination and, by implication at least, a defender of its particularistic interpretation of the faith and order of Christians. As Loren P. Beth has argued, the "designation of our problem as 'church and state' is incomplete and misleading" because "our conflict is not merely between two institutions, but between two sides of the individual—the political and the religious."[23]

To be sure, Jesus' admonition to "Render therefore to Caesar the things that are Caesar's, and to God the things that are God's" (Matt. 22:21) still suggests an admirable guideline. But in the democratic Republic the citizen, unlike his ancestor in the Roman Empire (whether citizen or not), cannot objectify "Caesar" as the coercive power from without or from above that imposes order on the society. For under what Tocqueville called the dogma of our democracy, that sovereignty resides in the people, the citizen participates in "Caesar" and the struggle between Caesar and God is internalized. As Albert G. Huegli noted, "In his role as a Christian the Christian citizen in a democracy confronts himself in his role as a citizen."[24] This is the main reason why designation of the issue as between church and state, which projects the struggle outward and into two institutions, is misleading and distracts attention from the nature of the real problem.

This, then, to adapt Gunnar Myrdal's observation respecting

what he called "the American Negro problem," is another "American dilemma." It is "a problem in the heart of the American," made manifest in the

> ever-raging conflict between, on the one hand, the valuations preserved on the general plane which we shall call the "American Creed," where the American thinks, talks, and acts under the influence of high national and Christian precepts, and, on the other hand, the valuations on the specific planes of individual and group living, where personal and local interests; economic, social, and sexual jealousies; considerations of community prestige and conformity; group prejudice against particular persons or types of people; and all sorts of miscellaneous wants, impulses, and habits dominate his outlook.[25]

It is on the level of what Myrdal calls "specific planes" that we observe the persistence of "sectarianism" which the thrust of the ecumenical and merger movements often brings to the surface.

I think I use the words *sectarian* and *sectarianism* with fair consistency and with a definiteness of meaning that I learned from those evangelical Protestant leaders of Europe and America who at the great meeting in London in August 1846 launched the Evangelical Alliances.

It has been said that next to the grace of God is the ability to see and make distinctions where differences exist. This is an aspect of the intellectual love of God. And those evangelicals saw a real difference, and made a sharp distinction, between "the church," a "denomination," and a "sect"—and between "denominationalism" and "sectarianism"—all key concepts, in the discussion of the matter before us, which today are often used interchangeably.

The phrase *the church* was recognized, not as a description of what was observed, but as a *theological assertion* of the unity of all believers in the "idea and purpose" of God, in "the mystical union" with Christ, and in "the willing and conscious bond of union" called "faith." The church, the body of Christ, is one: this was the primary premise of the inherited conceptual order which they brought to the observation of the new fact of division into numerous independent religious organizations.

The pressing question, then, was, Why the divisions? Because, as Charles Hodge, professor of theology at Princeton, explained in a classic statement in 1873, it is not promised that "they shall be perfect [and therefore one] in knowledge." It follows that "diversity of doctrine . . . among believers is unavoidable in our imperfect state," and diversity of doctrine has led to disagreements respecting proper forms which are institutionalized in the several separate organizations.[26] From this perspective, division into numerous groups is not a sin, as some ecumenical leaders today would have it.

In this conceptual context a denomination was seen as an organized group that, accepting these premises, recognized itself as a visible but finitely limited part of the church founded upon imperfect knowledge, apprehension, and exemplification of the gospel. A denomination did not make the claim exclusively to be the church. It did not absolutize or universalize any of the particularities that distinguished it from other Christian groups.

A sect was defined by these nineteenth-century evangelicals as a group that does make such claims—whether it be as small as "the society of Sandemanian Baptists [in New York], consisting of seven persons, two men and five women, who hold that they constitute the whole church in America,"[27] or as large as the Roman Catholic church with its millions of members. A sect based its exclusivistic claim, not on those elements it shared with all Christians, but upon those peculiarities of emphasis on doctrine and modes of practice which distinguished it from other Christians. It universalized its particularities and viewed observance of them as necessary for salvation. It exhibited, as one evangelical said, the very human tendency of each individual "at least in thought, to hold that Christendom, to be one, must be drawn within the circle of belief in which he dwells, and which he thinks to be the very citadel of the truth of God."[28] This was sectarianism.

Denominationalism, on the other hand, was conceived as that system wherein the church—the body of Christ—was divided into discrete bodies, each denominated by a different name. Recognition of the underlying unity of the church prevented any true denomination from making the absolutistic claim exclusively to be the church. Hence, as Philip Schaff noted in 1855:

> There is a difference between denominationalism and sectarianism. The former is compatible with true catholicity of spirit [and with religious freedom]; the latter is nothing but an extended selfishness, which crops out of human nature everywhere and in all ages and conditions of the church.[29]

Here in this movement, then, we see a vigorous attempt to reconcile an inherited conceptual order of Protestant Christendom with a new and different observed and experienced order, out of which was adumbrated a Christian theology in explanation and defense of pluralism.[30]

The denominational stance implies the eventual erosion of belief in the ultimate significance of the particularities of doctrine and practice that distinguish one Christian group from another.[31] A Presbyterian clergyman said as much in summarizing his understanding of the meaning of the organization of the Evangelical Alliances in 1846. A Christian, he said, must join a denomination, "for he is bound to belong to the Church visible, as well as to that which is invisible." But henceforth "let that connexion be on the maxim,—'Preference not exclusion.'" Exclusivistic claims were ruled out on the basis that perhaps "God can see a Christian where we cannot."[32] This is to say that a finite man must entertain the possibility that he and even his "church" may be wrong. This stance is an absolute necessity for real dialogue.

Obviously a revolutionary change in conceptual order is taking place when, for example, the mode of baptism, or the apostolic succession, or Presbyterian polity, is not defended on scriptural authority and/or tradition, but adhered to as a matter of preference or taste. For this means that a member's basis for choice between the "churches" is shifted out of the realm of authority and rational deduction into the realm of taste or aesthetics. That Episcopalian felt this who is alleged to have said, in a gross popularization of a profound point, that of course there are other routes to heaven, but no gentleman or lady would take them. The denominational stance implies this shift.

I think that practically all the pressures of the unfolding history-that-happens, the history that can be observed in the development of the United States, have been and are on the side of the denominational stance. This is what was inherent in principle from the beginning of America's "lively experiment." Philip Schaff saw more than a hundred years ago that

> America seems destined to be the Phoenix grave not only of all European nationalities, . . . but also of all European churches and sects, of Protestantism and Romanism. I cannot think, that any one of the present confessions and sects . . . will ever become exclusively dominant there; but rather, that out of the mutual conflict of all something wholly new will gradually arise.[33]

The thrust of our contemporary ecumenical movement is of the same nature. "The final and terrible difficulty," wrote its outstanding historian with what sounds like an echo of Schaff's view, is that Churches cannot unite, unless they are willing to die. In a truly united Church, there would be no more Anglicans or Lutherans or Presbyterians or Methodists. But the disappearance from the world of those great and honoured names is the very thing that many loyal churchmen are not prepared to face. Much has already been achieved. But until Church union clearly takes shape as a better resurrection on the other side of death, the impulse towards it is likely to be weak and half-hearted.[34]

This is to say that the ecumenical movement represents now, as did the evangelical movement of the nineteenth century, a real threat to the sectarian roots of the self-identity which has characterized every Christian group in the pluralistic society. Therefore resistance to it is commensurate with the sectarianism of a group. And this is why, while on what Myrdal calls the "general plane . . . of high . . . Christian precepts" there is much grand talk of ecumenism and church unity, when representatives of two or more religious groups meet eyeball-to-eyeball on the ecumenical or merger line they often exhibit an extreme sectarianism.[35]

Some examples drawn from a journalistic examination of church unity movements illustrate this. Roman Catholics, it was noted, now join Protestants "in confessing the 'sin' of Christian divisions, . . . and asking God to 'break our heart of stone and give us a heart able to repent.' "[36] It is recognized that "Protestant-Catholic unity can develop . . . only if both sides are receptive." I suppose that such "receptivity" means that each must be willing to surrender some of the particularistic forms that distinguish it. Granted that division is sinful, as many seem to assume, this would be tangible evidence of—fruit worthy of—such repentance as is prayed for, because it is their particularities (what some call their "distinctives") that divide the Christian groups one from another.

But *can* these groups give up any of their distinctive peculiarities? In one sense, by definiton *they* cannot, because for a group to relinquish what to it is a substantive point would be to lose its historical and present identity and become something different— to lose its life. So "both faiths remain adamant on matters of substance," apparently unmindful that "whoever would save his life will lose it" (Matt. 16:25). Roman Catholic leaders have insisted that their church will not yield on theological issues, for "there can be no compromise on . . . divinely revealed doctrine." A Protestant leader echoes, "We also are not interested in compromises." And W. A. Visser 't Hooft, at the time secretary-general of the World Council of Churches, declared that "no serious participant in our movement wants to give up his spiritual integrity and his real convictions."

Perhaps that Methodist bishop who is reported to have said that "the process . . . moves from acquaintance to acceptance to affiliation and finally to assimilation" spoke with candor what many unityists unconsciously felt. To assimilate means to digest, and while unity is a high and impeccable idea, the fear of being digested seems often to dampen enthusiasm at the crucial point. "I have found," said another Methodist bishop, "that many will shout 'hosanna' to the vision but cry out 'crucify it' when they see what it costs." Episcopalians seem most commonly to have counted the cost in advance and to have frankly stated the price they would not pay. Typically their representatives entered a six-denomination discussion with the flat declaration that their "delegation was required to insist on its views of the ministry." And one of their bishops blew old embers into flame by saying that "Only a jaundiced Puritan can fail to see the beauty of . . . the chain of hands down through the ages. . . . We must pool our riches," he explained, "and one of the riches we . . . have to offer is the apostolic succession." But to a Methodist this meant "admitting we've been illegitimate for 200 years" and, indicating that Methodists might resist having *their* "riches" dissolved in the Episcopalian's pool, he added, "Our success shows that we need more illegitimacy." Perhaps the layman who suggested that related denominations ought to get together "as fast as they can without waiting . . . [for the clergy to] settle knotty theological problems with remote denominations" did not understand the profound inertia lurking in such clerical jargon as "the chain of hands" and "illegitimacy."

As a layman I would have to admit that the particularities that form the foundation of sectarianism have become practically meaningless to me, and I suspect that my counterparts on the campuses and in the pews are legion. Laymen have been not just sprinkled with an ecumenical shower from above but soaked and agitated in the historical flood of religious pluralism until sectarianism has been washed out. They are ready to believe with Philip Schaff that something "wholly new will gradually arise." For them the pressing question is: "What is that 'common type of faith and life' that God has permitted to emerge out of the American experience of Christianity?" This, I think, is the primary question confronting the denominations today.

4

The "Nation with the
Soul of a Church"[1]

The apt phrase, "a nation with the soul of a church" was coined
by G. K. Chesterton in answer to his question, "What Is America?" the title of the autobiographical essay in which he relates how
he came to appreciate what the United States was all about.

The idea of the United States, Chesterton decided, was that of
an asylum—"a home for the homeless"—of all the world. What
made this country different was the "idea of making a new nation
literally out of [the people of] any old nation that comes along."[2]
Because every nation is a spiritual entity, it was implied that the
spiritual entity of this nation must include every religion that these
diverse people brought along.

The new nation was "conceived in liberty, and dedicated to the
proposition that all men are created equal." It was the idea of actually incarnating this "theory of equality" in the familiar practice
of a nation that Chesterton found unique about America—the in-
carnation of "the pure classic conception that no man must aspire
to be anything more than a citizen, and that no man shall endure
to be anything less."[3]

By the same token, vis-à-vis such a civil commonwealth, no religious sect must aspire to be anything more than equal with all the others, and none should endure to be anything less. The idea of actually incarnating this theory of the equality of all religious sects in relation to the civil authority is what was unique about the American experiment. The persistence of sectarianism indicates how reluctant religious leaders have been to accept *this* theory of equality in principle. But just as the ideal of America has been that "of moulding many peoples into the visible image of the citizen," so it was implied that the religious ideal was that of melding the many diverse sectarianisms into one cosmopolitan religion.

Here, in a series of broad generalizations, I shall try to picture the emergence and development of this theory of equality and its implications. We may begin with an examination of the nature of a nation, which suggests that America was less unique in Christendom than Chesterton might lead one to suppose.

In the fullness of time when Christianity was born, the Roman Empire was a fact of experience, and subtle philosophers "combining elements of Platonism with the tenets of the Stoics" had suggested the idea of the world as "a single city of God."[4] The experienced and conceptual orders insofar corroborated one another, "unity answered to unity." Then, as Ernest Barker argues,

> When the Emperor was worshipped as a manifest god and saviour by all his subjects, the society of the Empire became a quasi-religious society, cemented by a common allegiance which was also a common cult.[5]

In its conception of the church as a single, organic society which transcended and included "all earlier distinctions, whether of Jew and Gentile, or of Greek and barbarian, or of bond and free," Christianity represented its own ideal of a universal society permeated by the personal spirit of God. The "political world-society . . . possessed a universality which answered to the aspiring and universal genius of the early Church." In effect and, to be sure, with much searching, struggle and compromise, Christianity moved into the shell of the empire. The church "became a world-society co-extensive with the world-empire" and "Christianity became both a city of God in conception and an organized universal society in action." Thus it was that when "the Roman Empire vanished in the West: the Catholic society remained. . . . It was a fact, and not merely an idea: and yet it was also an idea, and not altogether a fact." For tribal societies with their particularistic tribal cults were being swept into the Catholic society before their people had fully absorbed, and been absorbed into, the true Catholic idea.

The nation as idea and fact sprang from those seeds of tribalism which germinated and were nourished in the soil of the Christian world-society. Nations emerged with the coincidence of a geographical center (e.g., London or Paris) and a strong political authority, usually a monarch or a line of monarchs, powerful and persuasive enough to become symbols of unity, order, and security. The tie that binds a nation together is "neither a physical fact of common blood [for "all are composite and heterogeneous"], nor a political structure of common law and order" as was, for example, the Roman Empire. National consciousness gradually emerged among the inhabitants of a territory around "a common allegiance, common memories, and a common tradition—a tradition of uniform law and government, uniform speech, a single literature, a common history."

A nation, then, "is what it is in virtue of a common mental substance resident in the minds of all its members—common hopes for the future, and, above all, a common and general will issuing from the common substance of memories, ideas and hopes."[6] John Wise, in his *Vindication of the Government of New England Churches* in 1717, echoes the then current view that with the compact by which government is formed, comes "that submission and union of wills by which a state may be conceived to be but one person." It is "a compound moral person, whose will (united by those compacts . . .) is the will of all . . . as though the whole state was now become but one man. . . ." And in this sense the compacts by which this state is created, "may be supposed, under God's providence, to be the divine fiat pronounced by God, 'Let us make man.' "[7] The similarity to the Christian conception of the church as the body of Christ is obvious. A nation, in brief, is "essentially a spiritual society," its soul created in the compact of the people.

But, and this is most important, unlike the empire and Catholic society, the nation "in its essence . . . was a negation of universality: it was a particularist society, confined to a given territory and peculiar to a given body of persons."

In this particularist "spiritual society" the Christian church with its concept of "the world-society" met "something new, and something different in kind from the Empire with which it had come to terms a thousand years before." The "struggles between kings and popes had been struggles . . . between rival authorities."[8] The struggles between the universal church and the nations were struggles between rival spiritual societies and, as such, a confrontation of rival theologies.

The emergence of the nations corresponds in time with the Reformation, so that concurrent with the fragmentation of the empire into nations came the fragmentation of the universal visible church into many particular churches. And in those areas where

Reformation churches were established (Scotland, England, Geneva, Holland, the principalities of North Germany, and Scandinavia) the nation assumed its own form of Christianity and established "a national form of religious organization" fusing "the spiritual tradition of the new and secular nation . . . with the spiritual tradition of the old and Christian society. . . ." Thus the essentially spiritual society of the nation was, in effect, Christianized by partially digesting into its spiritual core a particularized version of Christianity. For its people the nation became also their church, and the church became also their nation, church and nation being merely different perspectives on the one society to which they belonged. Such at least, says Ernest Barker, was the vision of Hooker and Laud in England where the identification was most complete, although never absolute.[9] It always stood under the judgment of the ancient and Catholic concept of universalism, and even while Laud and Charles I ruled it was being challenged in England by Nonconformists with a different view of the nature of a church and, consequently, of its relation to civil authority. It was the Nonconformist view, adapted to the American environment, that was to triumph and be assumed in the constitutional and legal structure of the United States.

By and large, the Reformation churches of the right-wing became the tribal cults of the emerging nations. And because Roman Catholicism via-à-vis these nation-churches also found its defenders in national societies, it likewise tended to assume characteristics of a tribal cult in those countries. During the last quarter of the sixteenth century, for example, it was clearly English-Protestantism versus Spanish-Catholicism.[10] And I suppose that Gallicanism means that the Catholic church in France was speaking to Rome with a decidedly French accent.

The extent to which the Roman Catholic church was "nationalized" in those countries where it remained dominant was revealed when the flood of immigrants poured into the United States from the several nations of Europe. Soon, says Monsignor John Tracy Ellis, they "completely overshadowed the native Catholics and gave to the Church a foreign coloring that at once baffled its friends and exasperated its enemies." But the "foreign coloring" was itself a coat of many different colors. In America, Ellis notes, the Roman Catholic church was made up of a "congeries of nationalities" who shared only their foreignness, and their Catholicism which (as Will Herberg has argued so persuasively) was but one element in the definition of their ethnic identity. The problem for Catholics in America was to mold this heterogeneous collection of nationals into one church. And it was because of that necessity, says Monsignor Ellis, that the Roman Catholic church in the United States "Willy-nilly . . . had [to] become catholic in the broadest sense. . . ."[11]

Because during the period following the Reformation it seemed sufficiently demonstrated that religious differences were a chief cause of internal dissension and international wars, the national ideal was religious uniformity institutionalized in an established church. Thus experience consolidated the nation-church ideal. In the Protestant England of Elizabeth I, to be a Roman Catholic was presumptive evidence of disloyalty to the nation and its monarch, as in Catholic France the reverse was the case.

Both Catholicism and Nonconformity refused "to accept the identification of religious and national society."[12] Lord Baltimore and Roger Williams, who founded the first colonies with religious freedom, had at least that much in common! But it would seem that the writings of those who assumed and accepted such identification are an unlikely place to go looking for a doctrine of the church which will enable the American people to understand their denominations in a land where religious pluralism has been a fact for three hundred years, where "*the* church" as such does not exist in visible institutional form, and where religious freedom has prevailed for about two centuries. Yet by and large, Americans of the theological revival evident since around 1930 who went looking for a "doctrine of the church" dug for historical roots primarily in the writings of representatives of the right-wing national church tradition. Twenty years ago I heard a scholar justify this limitation with the dogmatic declaration that the Baptists, for example, "never had a doctrine of the church." In one respect at least, I find myself in agreement with Harvey Cox:

> Our doctrines of the church have come to us from the frayed-out period of classical Christendom and are infected with the ideology of preservation and permanence. They are almost entirely past-oriented, deriving their authority from one or another classical period, from an alleged resemblance to some earlier form of church life, or from a theory of historical continuity. But this will no longer do.[13]

In my context, this will not do if we hope ever to understand the institutional forms of Christianity in the United States and/or the relation of the denominations which emerged out of the experience of Christianity in America to the civil authority of the nation. Thomas Jefferson spoke from experience, both when he commended the Baptists for their consistent advocacy of religious freedom, *and* when he said of the right-wing clergy of New England that "the advocate of religious freedom is to expect neither peace nor forgiveness from them."

But meanwhile the Reformers established the principle that the individual was justified by faith alone, which removed all human mediators between God and man and established a direct and immediate relation between the individual and God in Christ. While this obviously undermined the claim of the clergy of the visible church to be the sole mediators of eternal salvation, it tended also, though less obviously, to undermine the claim of civil rulers to be *"the* powers . . . ordained of God" of Romans 13:1. The result, noted by Philip Schaff, was that historically "with the universal priesthood comes also a corresponding universal kingship."[14] And Kierkegaard exclaimed, "Oh, Luther, Luther; your responsibility is great indeed, for the closer I look the more clearly do I see that you overthrew the Pope—and set the public on the throne."[15]

This development, this inversion in the conceptual order, laid the foundation for modern democracy—the idea that sovereignty, the power of God for the creation of ordered communities, lies in "the people" and is delegated by them to rulers responsible to them.

One sees this development taking place in the vicissitudes of that "due forme of government both civill and ecclesiastical" which those Puritans who established Massachusetts Bay Colony envisaged and attempted to bring into familiar and daily practice. They accepted without question what was then almost universally conceded in their England, that all government must be by the consent of the governed[16]—a concept which they subsumed under the traditional Jewish-Christian image of the covenant of God with his peculiar people. In their transitional conceptual order they merged the idea of the church as the tribal cult with that of the church as a gathered and covenanted people, and attempted to incarnate and preserve the idea in practice by the simple expedient of ruling that only church members could vote in the election of civil magistrates, who in turn were chosen only from among the Saints. Thus the gathered church was coextensive with the actual state, the laws of which, it was supposed, coincided with the laws of God. Hence outward obedience to the laws of the commonwealth, whether consciously and willingly as by the Saints, or reluctantly as by the unregenerate, was by definition outward conformity to the laws of God.

They described their church government as "mixt": in relationship to Christ its head, it was an absolute monarchy; in relationship to its officers who held direct subordinate power under Christ, it was an aristocracy; when viewed from the perspective of the members who also had their direct subordinate power under Christ, it was a democracy.[17] All the parts of their church government, they held, were exactly revealed in the Word of God, and evidence of a true work of grace in an individual's heart was found in his desire to consent to that church's support and discipline. The government of the church was by the consent of the governed, which consent they were enabled by grace to give.

Whatever one may think of their exegesis of Scripture and the conclusions respecting church government which they deduced therefrom, or of their actual practices, the important thing for the future was that *this church-state was a democracy of the Saints.* Obviously the whole structure rested upon the assumption that, within the judgment of charity, they could distinguish the Saints from the unregenerate with sufficient accuracy to guarantee the perpetuation of the rule of the Saints. And when confidence in that assumption was undermined, as it soon was when morality became indistinguishable from piety, the democracy of the Saints flowed out to embrace the whole community, to include all the people. At the same time, for the Biblical orientation of the original covenant was substituted the concept of "the law of nature"— of men in "the state of nature" endowed with natural rights common to all men whether religious or not. John Wise, in his *Vindication of the Government of the New England Churches,* while using all the traditional arguments from Scripture and the practice of the primitive church until the apostasy under Constantine, is most remembered for his Demonstration II, "From the Light of Nature." Here he argued that man is "a free-born subject under the crown of heaven, and owing homage to none but God himself." And since God has not ordained any "particular form of civil government" one concludes it "must . . . be the effect of human free-compacts and not of divine institution: it is the produce [*sic*] of man's reason, of human and rational combinations, and not from any direct orders of infinite wisdom. . . ."[18]

The founders of the United States accepted this view as axiomatic. It should not be forgotten that

> Our foundations were quarried not only from the legal ideas but also from the political, social, philosophical, scientific, and theological learnings of the eighteenth century, "the silver age of the Renaissance." All these were dominated by a belief in "the laws of nature and of nature's God." Faith in a "higher law," which had achieved a venerable place in the history of ideas through the speculations of jurists, monks, and scholars, burst forth toward the end of the eighteenth century into a fanatical creed that took over French and American liberal thinking and led in each case to a violent revolution.[19]

The course of history exhibits the slow, strong power of high generalities to get incarnated in actuality, and our institutions are primarily incarnations of the constellation of myths and ideas that dominated the thinking of the eighteenth century in which the nation was born.

Prominent in that constellation was the view that sovereign power lies in "the people," who by a first compact agree to have a government, and by a second compact agree upon the kind of government they want. In the founders' thinking, the unique opportunity they possessed was to actualize in practice what a long line of thinkers had conceived as proper government for men. The dissolution of the political bonds that had bound these people to the English state, proclaimed in the Declaration and made good by successful revolution, meant that the sovereign power was returned to the people who, by implication, desired a government more likely to secure their rights. Now the people could choose the kind of government they wanted, a choice that was exemplified in the acceptance of the Constitution.

There were certain "givens" in the situation which had to be recognized and accepted in framing the new government. Prominent among these "givens" was the fact that by the time the Constitutional Convention met, religious pluralism had been, willingly or grudgingly, accepted in every colony. Everywhere, religious uniformity had broken down, making the ideal of a national tribal cult institutionalized in one established church impossible. If there was to be a *United* States " 'there was no choice but to tolerate all Christian denominations, and forbear entering into the particular views of any,' " Robert Baird noted in 1845.[20] Vis-à-vis each of the many conflicting religious sects, the new nation's central authority had to be neutral, neither favoring nor hindering any sect's beliefs or practices except where the latter might violate socially acceptable conduct.

> The First Amendment was therefore to insure that no one powerful sect or combination of sects could use political or governmental power to punish dissenters whom they could not convert to their faith. Now as then, it is only by wholly isolating the state from the religious sphere and compelling it to be completely neutral, that the freedom of each and every denomination and of all nonbelievers can be maintained.[21]

It is worth repeating that such neutrality, which is often referred to as "secularization," is more accurately described as de-sectarianization of the civil authority.[22] Pluralism means many different sects, each a religious interest group, and civil neutrality is based on the recognition, as Reinhold Niebuhr put it, that "it is dangerous to give any interest group [in a nation] the monopoly to define the 'truth' " as was the practice in nations with established churches.[23]

Sectarians, and all advocates who cannot disentangle their particular religious forms from the universal essence of religion, are bound to argue that this means that the civil government is unreligious, or irreligious, even antireligious—which is what they commonly mean by "secular." This is to confuse antisectarianism with antireligious. At the time, and from his point of view, Bishop Hughes of New York was right in the early 1840s when he said, "Take away the distinctive dogmas of the Catholics, the Baptists, the Methodists, the Presbyterians, and so on, and you have nothing left but deism,"[24] and deism, he thought, was itself sectarian. For the "deism" exhibited in the Declaration was a positive religious teaching with, as G. K. Chesterton noted, a lucid and even dogmatic theology.

It was a cosmopolitan, inclusive, universal theology. The founders, typical eighteenth-century intellectuals oriented to the actualities of the American scene, were cosmopolitans nationally and religiously. They were cosmopolitans nationally in the sense that Franklin meant when he said, ". . . a Philosopher may set his foot anywhere on . . . [the world's] surface, and say, 'This is my country.' "[25] So such a Philosopher might have entered any church, as Franklin symbolically did by contributing his mite to each, and declare, "This is my church."

Because it is so commonly supposed that the theology of these men like Franklin was *syncretistic*—that is, a common core made up by combining a heterogeneous set of discrete tenets collected from all the sects—it is worth emphasizing that this was not the case. Their view might more precisely be called *synergistic,* which designates the simultaneous action of separate agencies working in combination to effect an end. When Franklin spoke of "the essentials of every religion" he added that these were "to be found in all the religions we had in our country" though in each "mix'd with other articles" peculiar to that sect. This is not to create a syncretistic common core, but to plumb for the universal which is dressed and disguised in the particularities of doctrine and practice that distinguish one sect from another. This conception enabled them to distinguish between the substance of religion, and its forms exemplified in sectarian tenets and observances. They were aware, in Whitehead's words, that "Religious ideas represent highly specialized forms of general notions"[26] and in their theologizing they plumbed for the "general notions."

When Franklin and those of like mind listened to a sectarian preacher, they might hear through the particular forms of his pronouncements "the essentials of every religion"—the substance of all religion. Although the preacher might preach on the specific plane, Franklin might listen on the general plane; while the preacher preached specific notions, Franklin might be reminded of the high generalities implicit in and behind the speaker's sectarian presentation. This is not *syncretism* but the idea that the universal is encapsulated in the particular and unique.

This conception, as the founders well realized, is eminently compatible with actual religious freedom and consequent legal pluralism in a *common*wealth. It provides a basis for a positive explanation and defense of religious pluralism which does not necessarily undermine belief in the efficacy of sectarian forms to express the universal. Indeed it encourages the free, open, and uncurbed proclamation of all sectarian specific notions respecting, in Madison's words, "the duty which we owe to our creator, and the manner of discharging it." It encourages even vehement conflict of opinion between them on the premises stated by Jefferson in the "Act for Establishing Religious Freedom in Virginia":

> that truth [which is universal] is great and will prevail if left to herself, that she is the proper and sufficient antagonist to error, and has nothing to fear from the conflict, unless . . . disarmed of her natural weapons, free argument and debate, errors ceasing to be dangerous when it is permitted freely to contradict them.

On this basis religious pluralism and conflict between the sects is promoted under the aegis of a *neutral* civil authority which limits the conflict to "reason and persuasion . . . [as] the only practicable instruments"[27] for mining the universal truth out of the diversity of opinions that prevails. In this situation each sect, whether knowingly or not, is communicating to its members through its particular forms the universal truth in which all religions meet. Believing this, Jefferson could say of Virginia's neighbors, Pennsylvania and New York, that there "Religion is well supported; of various kinds, indeed, but all good enough. . . ."[28] That somehow they are "all good enough" is plowed into our tradition.

Of course, it is important to distinguish between the universal those eighteenth-century cosmopolitans plumbed for and the specific notions they came up with in defining its content.[29]

Those were notions respecting the content of the universal, to which anyone may legitimately oppose and argue for another constellation of specific notions. But if and when he does so, he should realize that on the plane of high generality he is in agreement with the sentiment implicit in the whole American experience that the universal, however latent, is encapsulated in the particular forms of the sects.

There is today among Christians a fine flurry of thinking and activity to "tangibilicate"—to borrow that wonderful word from Father Divine—the answer to the prayer of Jesus "that they all may be one . . . that they also may be one in us . . ." (John 17:21). I suppose that this implies the eventual shedding of all belief that any sectarian particularity is in itself of ultimate significance. The goal of Oneness implies a common universal principle inherent in all sects, in which their sectarian identity is seen to be at most penultimate. But I have found few real attempts to define the substance of that universal in the form of specific notions respecting its content. Indeed, most churchmen today, unlike their evangelical grandfathers in the nineteenth century and their rationalistic great-grandfathers in the eighteenth, seem commonly to be frightened away from this attempt by fears of a loss of sectarian identity and the bogey of a "common core" of religion. Nevertheless the ideal, the aspiration, persists. In this connection I quote at some length what seems to have been Paul Tillich's final conclusion, stated in his book *Christianity and the Encounter of the World Religions:*

> Does our analysis demand either a mixture of religions or the victory of one religion, or the end of the religious age altogether? We answer: None of these alternatives! A mixture of religions destroys in each of them the concreteness which gives it its dynamic power. The victory of *one* religion would impose a particular religious answer on all other particular answers. The end of the religious age— one has already spoken of the end of the Christian or the Protestant age—is an impossible concept. The religious principle cannot come to an end. For the question of the ultimate meaning of life cannot be

silenced as long as men are men. Religion cannot come to an end, and a particular religion will be lasting to the degree in which it negates itself as a religion. Thus Christianity will be a bearer of the religious answer as long as it breaks through its own particularity.[30]

Tillich's view seems to me implicit in the whole American experience with religious pluralism.

This sentiment permeates our tradition until, as Chesterton said, America is "a cosmopolitan commonwealth."[31] This means that its synergistic cosmopolitanism lies at the heart of its nationalism—that a definitive element of the spiritual core which identifies it as a nation is the conception of a universal principle which is thought to transcend and include all the national and religious particularities brought to it by the people who come from all the world to be "Americanized." America, Philip Schaff noted, from Broadway in New York to the markets of San Francisco, presents "an ethnographic panorama," but

> what is most remarkable is, that over this confused diversity there broods after all a higher unity, and that in this chaos of people the traces of a specifically American national character may be discerned.[32]

What is the nature of that brooding "higher unity"? A somewhat plausible answer was suggested by a bright young student from Germany who, to improve his understanding of religion in America, had attended services in many different churches. He reported to me that what struck him most was that the only common symbol he found in *all* of them was the United States flag. The fact that in so many of our churches the flag of the United Nations is now displayed beside the flag of the United States suggests the belief that in this nation it is not incongruous or unpatriotic to symbolize the universality inherent in its spiritual core. This stance originated with the Republic. In the First Federalist Paper Alexander Hamilton, arguing for acceptance of the Constitution, described the venture as an experiment to find out if men could have government by reflection and choice. Thus considered, he argued, the inducements of "philanthropy" (love for mankind) are added to those of "patriotism" (love for country) to back the experiment, because the results of the experiment will be of consequence for all humanity.

The United States is a nation. As a nation it has its spiritual core of which the flag is the symbol.[33] To be sure "nations are human societies, created in time, with the imperfections of the temporal." But we must disabuse ourselves of the notion that therefore "nations are also secular—at least in that sense of the word in which it is used as the antithesis and the negation of the religious."[34] No nation can be called "merely secular, or altogether earthly."[35] It is for this reason that nationalism, as the common sense of distinctive identity, is not necessarily absolutistic or idolatrous. It depends upon the spiritual core, the religion of the nation in question.

Religion, of course, is expressed in culturally rooted and conditioned language. And, as Tillich put it, "language is the expression of man's freedom from the given situation and its demands. It gives him universals in whose power he can create worlds above the given world. . . ."[36] The "worlds above the given world" are pictured in the great mythologies or dramas of the religions, which hold before the people the ideals and aspirations which define their sense of destiny and purpose. Man, says Whitehead, is the animal that can cherish aspirations, which is to be religious, to be committed to an ideal world beyond the present world and to the incarnating of that ideal world in actuality. The religion of this, our Republic, is of this nature. Therefore to be committed to that religion is not to be committed to this world as it is, but to a world as yet above and beyond it to which this world ought to be conformed. The "American religion," contrary to Will Herberg's much popularized misunderstanding, is *not* "the American way of life"[37] as we know and experience it, any more than the Christian faith *is* the way of life that ordinary professing "Christians" commonly exemplify in their everyday activities.

To be sure, all "Great ideas enter into reality with evil associates and with disgusting alliances. But the greatness remains, nerving the race in its slow ascent."[38]

Seen thus the religion of the Republic is essentially prophetic, which is to say that its ideals and aspirations stand in constant judgment over the passing shenanigans of the people, reminding them of the standards by which their current practices and those of their nation are ever being judged and found wanting. One illustration is sufficient—an extract from the *Manila Times,* quoted in *The Christian Century,* March 2, 1966:

> It is no wonder that America, with every passing year, seems to have fewer and fewer friends in Asia. For, despite the ideals that once made America great and the burning words of quality [equality] and freedom that have made the US declaration of independence a beacon to all the world, these ideals are betrayed and the inspiring testament of the past confounded by the actuations of the higher-pressure business lobbies that now manipulate decisions in Old Foggy Bottom and around Capitol Hill. The American Eagle today brings with it, not a pledge of justice and fair play, but a 20th-century version of gunboat diplomacy dedicated to the protection of US big business.[39]

Is not this "prophetic"?

It seems very commonly supposed that this that I call the religion of the Republic means worship of the state or nation. My hunch is that this supposition is rooted in the general fact that the minds of so many American biblical scholars and theologians have been formed by European biblical and theological scholarship, which has largely dominated our theological education for one hundred years. At least in my experience most of the seminary graduates who have come to me for graduate work in American church history confess that they know practically nothing about the American experience of Christianity and its consequent modes of thinking and acting.

Professor Joseph Haroutunian, in commenting on this in a very perceptive article called "Theology and American Experience," argued that European modes of thought have not "struck a genuinely responsive chord in the mind of the American Christian."

> European philosophies and their logics . . . could not be readily naturalized in America. While professional theologians lived off European theology, the American Christian tried to get along with a minimum of intellectual discipline. When the latter thought, they did so, to a large measure, as Europeans, arguing for natural or revealed theology, or both; and they lived with a minimum of logic, going by some undisciplined if pious pragmatism which made shambles both of faith and of practice. Thus theology and American experience have been perennially at odds, and the Church in America has had to live to a large extent without the benefit of logic.[40]

What is at issue here is the conception of the intellectual quest itself, and the relation of the theologian to the concrete forms of the visible church of which he is supposedly a responsible member and articulate spokesman. My view is, in Whitehead's words, that "No religion can be considered in abstraction from its followers, or even from its various types of followers."[41] It follows that the task of theology should be to supply a "great intellectual construction explanatory of . . . [the] modes of understanding" which actually characterize a concrete visible church or denomination, and how those modes grew out of the peculiar experience of that group in history.

Is it not the case that many of the great seminal theologians of Christendom have combined in their persons—as did men as far apart and different as Augustine and Jonathan Edwards—the offices of theologian and ecclesiastical administrator? Consequently most of their theological works were, in the grand old phrase, to explain and defend the concrete modes of thinking and practice that actually characterized their groups. But in America theology has become a specialized discipline among several others, while the study and explanation of the visible church institutions has largely become the domain of historians, anthropologists and sociologists whose findings are about as distant from the center of the theologian's interest as are the actual faith and practice of church members and parish ministers.

In this context it is not difficult to understand why the contention that the religion of our Republic means worship of the state or nation goes, with a few notable exceptions, unchallenged. I would not be understood to argue that it is the best, or even a viable, religious stance for our day. But I would argue that one most constant strand in its theology has been the assertion of the primacy of God over all human institutions.

From John Cotton, who argued from this premise that all power that is on earth must be limited, to Mr. Justice Clark's assertion in the Schempp and Murray decision that we "are a religious people whose institutions presuppose a Supreme Being"[42] and Dwight Eisenhower's dictum that our institutions make no sense except in the context of religious faith, the idea has been plowed into our tradition. James Madison in his *Memorial and Remonstrance on the Religious Rights of Man* (1784) stated the implication clearly:

Before any man can be considered a member of civil society, he must be considered as a subject of the governor of the universe; and if a member of civil society, who enters into any subordinate association must always do it with a reservation of his duty to the general authority, much more must every man who becomes a member of any particular civil society do it *with the saving his allegiance to the universal sovereign.* We maintain, therefore, that in matters of religion no man's right is abridged by the institution of civil society. . . .

In 1946 Mr. Justice Douglas, writing the opinion in the Girourd case,[43] reasserted the same premise:

The victory for freedom of thought recorded in our Bill of Rights recognizes that in the domain of conscience there is a moral power higher than the State. Throughout the ages men have suffered death rather than subordinate their allegiance to God to the authority of the State. Freedom of religion guaranteed by the First Amendment is the product of that struggle.

Abraham Lincoln, who has seemed to me the most profound and representative theologian of the religion of the Republic, drew upon the universal element brought to him by the Jewish-Christian tradition for an understanding of the concrete events of the Civil War. "The war came," he said, and

Both [sides] read the same Bible and pray to the same God, and each invokes His aid against the other. It may seem strange that any men should dare ask a just God's assistance in wringing their bread from the sweat of other men's faces, but let us judge not, that we be not judged. The prayer of both could not be answered. That of neither has been answered fully. The Almighty has His own purposes. . . .

Fondly do we hope, fervently do we pray, that this mighty scourge of war may speedily pass away. Yet, if God wills that it continue until all the wealth piled up by the bondsman's two hundred and fifty years of unrequited toil shall be sunk, and until every drop of blood drawn with the lash shall be paid by another drawn with the sword, as was said three thousand years ago, so still it must be said "the judgments of the Lord are true and righteous altogether."

How can anyone suppose that Madison and Lincoln and Douglas and Eisenhower in these representative pronouncements represented an idolatrous worship of the nation, or the civil state, or of "the American Way of Life"?

Only when we realize the nature of the religion of the Republic can we begin to understand the nature of the struggle between sectarian Christianity and "Americanism," which is commonly confused by calling it a struggle between church and state, and discussing it under the categories applicable to other nations and a bygone period. "There is no such thing, organizationally, as the American church in the singular," to quote John E. Smylie's article, "National Ethos and the Church."[44] Traditionally the struggles between church and state were struggles between two institutionalized authorities. But in the United States the contest between what is commonly called church and state is actually between the one coherent, institutionalized civil authority, and about three hundred collectively incoherent religious institutions whose claims tend to cancel each other out.[45] And the primary conflicts have not been and are not now between the civil authority and the "churches," but between competing religious groups themselves. Because the civil authority has had to adjudicate these differences when they threatened to disrupt civil order, it was forced to become "neutral"—neither aiding nor hindering any religious group.

I conclude that what is commonly called the relation between church and state in the United States ought to be resolved into the theological issue beween the particularistic theological notions of the sects and the cosmopolitan, universal theology of the Republic. In the early days of the Republic, during the period of the French Revolution and the rise of the Jeffersonian party, leading defenders of orthodox Christianity so defined the issue.[46] In their terms it was the issue between revealed and natural religion. But in the heat of controversy they lost sight of the theological issue[47] —which was never fully discussed on its merits—and defended revealed religion functionally, arguing that it was the only sure ground for morality, upon which in turn stable government rested. They lumped all kinds and shades of dissent from their particularistic Christian views under the catch-all term "infidelity." And "infidelity," Timothy Dwight proclaimed, was a plan "for exterminating Christianity" which "presents no efficacious means of restraining Vice, or promoting Virtue, but on the contrary encourages Vice and discourages Virtue." Indeed, he thought, "So evident is the want of morals on the part of Infidels, in this country, generally, that to say 'A man is an Infidel' is understood, of course, as a declaration that he is a plainly immoral man." Therefore, he continued,

> Infidelity, naturally and necessarily, becomes, when possessed of the control of national interests, a source of evils so numerous, and so intense, as to compel mankind to prefer any state to those evils.[48]

On this basic argument the victory for Christianity over "infidelity" was won during the early days of the Republic. Infidelity, said Roger Sherman of Connecticut, ceased to be respectable. Indeed it did. But this says nothing about the intellectual merits of Timothy Dwight's representative defense of Christianity, or the intellectual merits of the "infidel" position. It did effectively sidetrack the theological issue for more than a century—indeed, it still does, until as Martin E. Marty argues in his book, *The Infidel* . . . , we are in danger of going through the whole process again, substituting for that era's "infidelity" the current catch-all term "secularism."[49]

We have noted G. K. Chesterton's suggestion that the United States is a nation with the soul of a church. Now, having placed this suggestion in a broad context, and canvassed some of its implications, we may note how and why in a very real sense the nation for many Americans came to occupy the place in their lives that traditionally had been occupied by the church. Here I find the argument of John E. Smylie in his article, "National Ethos and the Church"[50] quite convincing.

Religious freedom means pluralism. Pluralism means denominationalism and sectarianism. And, says Mr. Smylie, "this denominational experience has been devastating for attempts in American Protestantism to understand the church theologically." For Americans

> The denominational church, as they saw it, was not for them the New Israel of God's elect. It was a voluntary society, perhaps the most important among others, but hardly the organ through which God made his ultimate historical demands and offered his fullest earthly rewards.

And under religious freedom, because no denomination could plausibly claim to be, or to function as, "the church" in the new nation, *"the nation came more and more so to function."*

The easy theological merging of evangelical Protestantism with the religion of the Republic, and the concurrent merging of the traditional conception of the function (or purpose) of the church with that of the nation, is clearly seen in Lyman Beecher's sermon of 1827:

> Indeed, if it had been the design of heaven to establish a powerful nation in the full enjoyment of civil and religious liberty, where all the energies of man might find scope and excitement, on purpose to show the world by experiment, of what man is capable . . . where

could such an experiment have been made but in this country, . . .
the light of such a hemisphere shall go up to heaven, it will throw
its beams beyond the waves—it will shine into the darkness there,
and be comprehended; it will awaken desire, and hope, and effort,
and produce revolutions and overturnings, until the world is free.
. . . Floods have been poured upon the rising flame, but they can no
more extinguish it than they can extinguish the flames of Aetna. Still
it burns, and still the mountain heaves and murmurs; and soon it will
explode with voices, and thunderings, and great earthquakes. Then
will the trumpet of jubilee sound, and earth's debased millions will
leap from the dust, and shake off their chains, and cry, "Hosanna to
the Son of David."[51]

For Beecher, as for many of his contemporaries, the Republic
had become the ark of God's redemptive work in the world.
Passionately Protestant and Puritan though he was, he apparently
saw no incongruity in this position[52]—because, I think, Protestantism had become for him a principle of high generality which,
he thought, permeated and was being incarnated in the democratic
institutions of the Republic.

Again, as when reflecting upon the eighteenth-century Rational-
ists' position, we must be careful to distinguish between the universal that Beecher plumbed for and the specific notions he came
up with in defining its content. What those specific notions were
need not concern us here. We are concerned to note that for
Beecher, and I think he was fairly typical, the nation was assuming
the traditional function of the church as he struggled to harmonize
his inherited conceptual order with his religious experience as
American.

"Thus," says John E. Smylie, "American Protestantism endowed
the nation with churchly attributes, with three theological notes in
particular."

(1) ". . . the nation emerged as the primary agent of God's meaningful activity in history."[53] For example, when Lyman Beecher wrote *A Plea for the West* in 1835, he was convinced that "the millennium would commence in America" where "by the march of revolution and civil liberty, the way of the Lord is to be prepared," and from this "nation shall the renovating power go forth." Only America can provide the "physical effort and pecuniary and moral power to evangelize the world."[54]

(2) ". . . the nation became the primary society in terms of which individual Americans discovered personal and group identity." This, of course, is what so struck Will Herberg, who popularized in his *Protestant, Catholic, Jew* the mistaken notion that this was something that happened only in the twentieth century.

(3) "As the nation became the primary community for fulfilling historic purposes and realizing personal identity" it also assumed "a churchly function in becoming the community of righteousness"—which Abraham Lincoln clearly compared to the church when he told an audience in Indianapolis on February 11, 1861, that "when the people rise in masses in behalf of the Union and the liberties of their country, truly may it be said, 'The gates of hell shall not prevail against them.' "[55]

However much one may quarrel with Mr. Smylie's specific notions and the illustrations I have provided for them, I think his high generality must stand in substance.

What outstanding function did the Republic, conceived as "the primary agent of God's meaningful activity in history" perform vis-à-vis the many religious sects? Primarily, I think, the Republic's neutral civil authority set limits on the absolutistic tendencies inherent in every religious sect, preventing any one of them, or any combination of them, from gaining, or regaining, a monopoly on the definition of truth, and imposing its particular forms on all the people. The Bill of Rights and its application has prevented any sect, or combination of sects, from monopolizing the Word of God, and insofar kept them from becoming heteronomous in the society. This is the "neutral" civil authority's primary contribution. Sectarianism means that each sect wants its particular forms to be imposed as God's will on all people. The result is that today dogmatic insistence on the ultimate significance of any sect's particular tenets or observances seems to have reached the vanishing point except in citadels of impregnable isolation from the currents moving in the unfolding history of our world. Richard Cardinal Cushing, in a statement which exhibited the sincerity and "Christlike charity" for which he pleaded, told how he

> came to recognize that the differences between Catholics and Protestants in America were not so much religious as they were social and cultural. The differences in faith did not divide us so much as the ethnic differences of our parents and grandparents. I discovered that what the ecumenists today call "nontheological factors" were isolating us and setting Catholic against Protestant and Protestant against Catholic more than our doctrines.[56]

It was the civil authority that limited the conflicts between the religious groups in accordance with Jefferson's plea that "reason and persuasion" were "the only practicable instruments." And after more than two hundred years of such limitation, leaders in the churches discovered "dialogue," and in the twentieth century made a shining new virtue out of what civil authority began to force upon them in the seventeenth century. It seems to me that civil authority has been the most consistent and powerful of the "nontheological" factors that have pressed ecclesiastics into what Cardinal Cushing called "this . . . great and wonderful thing" that "we are talking to each other as Christians, as brothers." Theologically I am inclined to agree with him that this is a sign that the Holy Ghost is moving in our midst, is jolting us out of our smug and self-made ghettoes and pushing us toward the unity that Our Lord wills, for which He prayed on the night before He died.[57]

But it seems to me that the primary instrument used by the Holy Ghost to administer that "jolting" in the United States has been the "neutral" civil authority.

Of course, when this or any nation assumes the traditional garb of the church it is in danger of becoming heteronomous vis-à-vis other peoples and nations—asserting that they "must be subjected to a law [our law], strange and superior" though it may be to them.[58] One of the clearest exhibitions of a heteronomous attitude in this nation is found in Josiah Strong's book, *Our Country*. Strong argued that the Anglo-Saxon, as the representative in history of "civil liberty" and "pure *spiritual* Christianity," was "divinely commissioned to be, in a peculiar sense, his brother's keeper." Therefore "it is chiefly to the English and American peoples that we must look for the evangelization of the world . . . that all men may be lifted up into the light of the highest Christian civilization." Add to these considerations, he continued, the fact of our "rapidly increasing strength in modern times, and we have well-nigh a demonstration" that God is "not only preparing in our Anglo-Saxon civilization the die with which to stamp the people of the earth, but . . . [is] also massing behind that die the mighty power with which to press it." In brief, he concluded that "God with infinite wisdom and skill" is preparing our civilization to "impress its institutions upon mankind. . . ."[59]

The theology of the synergistic and theonomous religion of the Republic stands against this idolatrous tendency equally with Christianity, and Christians—even if they cannot Christianize it— might well be advised to recognize a potential ally. Judging from the past experience of the Christian church, one may doubt that any stand will be effective. For, to quote Albert Camus,[60] as in the medieval church the efficacy of the limit in itself, born in the universality of the Christian religion, was undermined, and the church "made increasing claims to temporal power and historical dynamism," so the Republic is likely to follow in the church's footsteps. And if sectarians continue to undermine rather than understand the religion of the Republic, it is likely that the nation will become increasingly heteronomous as the church did. But the limit born in the religion of the Republic is not likely to be undermined by increasing "secularism" any more than was the limit born in the religion of the Catholic society. The gates of hell have never prevailed against the church's vision of the universal. But religious particularity possessed of coercive power has.

Sectarianism, religious or national, is a greater threat than secularism or outright atheism, because, as the story of religious persecutions reminds us, when it comes in the guise of "the faith once delivered to the saints" it may legitimate terrible tyrannies. The primary religious concern in our nation must be to guard against national idolatry; against the state becoming God; against the Republic assuming a heteronomous stance vis-à-vis other nations. The founders sought to incarnate such a guard in the legal system of the new nation, the spiritual core of which is a theonomous cosmopolitanism. The constitutional structure was designed eventually to deny the traditional resort to coercive power to every religious sect, while protecting the right of each freely to compete openly with all the others. In this situation the sects "correct one another" for the civil authority by curbing all of them, encourage each to tell "the other that he is not God."[61] And under constitutional protection each individually, or all with one voice, have the right and ought constantly to remind all civil servants of this salutary principle.

The Christian vision of universalism slumbered within the sects until it was, largely in spite of them, incarnated in a religiously pluralistic commonwealth. Then the heteronomous sects, compelled by law to live side by side in overt peace, discovered that the limitation of their conflicts to reason and persuasion was a viable path to union, that such dialogue was a Christian virtue. May we not dream with generations of Americans that our commonwealth is the bearer in history of a political cosmopolitanism which may someday be incarnated in world institutions that will compel the now absolutistic nations also to live together in overt peace under recognized law until the necessity is metamorphosed into an ideal, and its practice into a virtue? Christians have had centuries of experience with this kind of transformation. Lincoln, while exposed to the temptations of possibly unlimited power, gave us an example of an individual who refused to be God, and appealed to our better natures to cherish and preserve the right of each to tell the other "that he is not God." He called it "the last, best hope of earth"—fragile as all hopes are—which we may "nobly save or meanly lose."

5

Neither Church nor State: Reflections on James Madison's "Line of Separation"[1]

It is common these days to use the term "church-state" to embrace all questions that arise under our Constitution respecting religious freedom, the relation of law and religion, and the relation of churches and governments. Although this terminology has its usefulness as a shortcut and as a symbol of current problems, it suffers from weaknesses and inadequacies. Church-state terminology comes to us from Europe and recalls a background which is quite unlike the American scene. It had its origin in a time when the church was indeed a single monolithic Church and government power was centered in a single ruler. It is inadequate to describe the American situation because of both the multitude of churches in this country and the dispersion of governmental power among the federal government, the states, and the local communities.[2]

In 1832 James Madison, after surveying the consequences in America of rejecting the long-standing dogma that "religion could not be preserved without the support of Government nor Government be supported without an established religion," wrote that he had to admit . . . that it may not be easy, in every possible case, to trace the line of separation between the rights of religion and the Civil authority with such distinctness as to avoid collisions & doubts on unessential points. The tendency to a usurpation on one side or the other, or to a corrupting coalition or alliance between them, will be best guarded against by an entire abstinance of the Government from interference in any way whatever, beyond the necessity of preserving public order, & protecting each sect against trespasses on its legal rights by others.[3]

It is unfortunate that the phrase Thomas Jefferson had used thirty years before in his letter to the Danbury (Connecticut) Baptist Association—"a wall of separation between church and state" —became almost universally known and used while Madison's more accurate terminology was forgotten. For Jefferson's words have been the source of much confusion and conflict because they have helped to perpetuate thinking about the situation in the United States with the traditional concepts of "church" and "state" which are really not applicable to the experienced order of Americans. And the reference to a "wall" conjures up the image of something quite tangible and solid, which was built once and for all in the beginning.

Madison's words—"the line of separation between the rights of religion and the Civil authority"—are much more precisely descriptive. For while there are religions, or "sects" as he called them, in the United States, there is no "church" in the traditional institutional sense. And while there is "Civil authority," there is no "state" in the meaning of the word during the centuries when national religious uniformity was the ideal and establishments existed. And Madison's word "line," unlike Jefferson's "wall," does not conjure up the image of a solid and unchanging structure built by the founders, but rather, "the path of a moving point, thought of as having length but not breadth," as my dictionary explains it. Further, the concept of a "line," unlike that of "wall," permits one to think of a point constantly moving, and even zigzagging, and therefore, as Madison noted, not always easy to trace "with such distinctness as to avoid collisions & doubts. . . ."

If we think of the American situation with Jefferson's concepts of "church," "state," and a "wall," the image conjured up is of two distinct and settled institutions in the society once and for all time separated by a clearly defined and impregnable barrier which has solid foundations in the Constitution. It is in this context that "ignorant armies clash by night," and also by day.

But if we think of the American situation with Madison's concepts of religious "sects," "Civil authority," and a "line" between them, the image is fluid, its elements constantly changing shape and moving into different relationships with each other. Religious "sects" may and have appeared in hundreds of different forms, and "Civil authority" under our constitutional federalism may wear hundreds of different masks. In the beginning no one knew, or could know, just where the line between them was or would be because no one could anticipate the multitudinous institutional forms of religion or the numerous masks of civil authority that would appear and because there were practically no precedents to serve as guidelines.

If we think with Jefferson's concepts, the image is of two antagonistic parties in the society, the one defending, the other attacking and attempting to tear down, a "wall." Each might take his slogan from Robert Frost's "Mending Wall." The defender of the wall with his father image of Jefferson

> . . . will not go behind his father's saying,
> And he likes having thought of it so well
> He says again, "Good fences make good neighbors."

The attacker of the wall, commonly unreflectively accepting the concepts developed in his religious tradition in the good old days before freedom and pluralism were permitted, stubbornly reiterates,

> Something there is that doesn't love a wall,
> That wants it down. . . .

If we think with Madison's concepts, we are launched, all together as Americans, on a common quest to find out where the line or lines may be between ecclesiastical bodies and between one or more of the forms of ecclesiastical bodies and one or more of the current masks of "Civil authority."

The Constitution and First Amendment laid down as guidelines very general, abstract principles in terms of no religious test for national office, no "establishment of religion," and no prohibition of the "free exercise thereof." But what these abstract principles would mean in practice no one could anticipate. That was left to be determined only as specific questions arose—justiciable issues under the rules of the game. Some of the questions have been: Do they mean that a state may not finance through taxation bus transportation to parochial schools, or textbooks, or lunches for children in such schools? Do they mean that a state may not appropriate money raised by taxation for the construction of buildings for a denominational college? Do they mean that I may not handle poisonous snakes as an act of worship although I think God commands it? Do they mean that I may not refuse a blood transfusion for my child when the men in white deem it necessary to save his life although I believe it is forbidden by God? Do they mean that a majority in a school district may institute its forms of religious exercises in the public schools? Do they mean that a child may refrain from participation in the salute to the flag because to him it is an act of idol worship forbidden by God?

All of these specific questions have been raised by persons with "standing," and dealt with one way or another in court decisions arrived at through the observance of elaborately defined legal procedures, which are part of the rules of the game we are playing for the high stakes of freedom.

I suppose that to most of us who are without legal training the word "decision" has connotations of definiteness and finality. At least it took some time for me to realize that a court decision in the United States is never the last word on the point at issue. But if we think of a particular Supreme Court decision with Jefferson's concept of a "wall" in mind, the decision is likely to be imaged as another large stone well-mortared into a solid barrier. However, if we think of a particular decision with Madison's concept of a "line" in mind, it is apt to be imaged as only a temporary point where the line appeared to a majority of the Justices to be at the moment.

A decision is never absolutely final. "The Federal constitution," as Mr. Justice Douglas once put it, "is not a code, but a rule of action—a statement of philosophy and point of view, a summation of general principles, a delineation of the broad outlines of a regime which the Fathers designed for us."[4] The work of the Supreme Court is the translation of these general principles "into concrete constitutional commands"[5]—"the application of universal principles to the endless and infinitely varied concrete instances that occur in the real world."[6] Further, almost every specific issue can be looked at from the perspective of "more than one so-called principle."[7] This means that every case involves "arguable controversies, problems of judgment and choice on which reasonable men can disagree and reasonable Justices of the Supreme Court of the United States divide five to four, or six to three, or in some other ratio."[8]

Again, unlike the practice in most other nations, the dissenting as well as the majority opinions are published. The dissenter, of course, "strives to undermine the Court's reasoning and discredit its results," and, compared to the spokesman of the court, he is "irresponsible" and can be freer and more vivid in expression. Consequently even careful study of a decision may leave one puzzled about "whether the majority opinion meant what it seemed to say or what the minority said it meant."[9] For this reason a decision where there are dissenting opinions may provide no sound basis for predicting where the next point in the line will be located.

A case always involves a conflict of interests between two parties in the society. Because of the way the Supreme Court operates, the issues that it takes up are commonly those on which parties in the society are hotly divided. The Justices, quite aware of the practical consequences and in the midst of all the ambiguities, must within a reasonable time come to a definite decision respecting which party wins and which loses. This, as Mr. Justice Frankfurter said, is "for any conscientious judge . . . the agony of his duty."[10]

So we return to Madison's concept of the "line" which Chief Justice Hughes once used in summarizing the situation:

> All rights tend to declare themselves absolute to their logical extreme. Yet all in fact are limited by the neighborhood of principles of policy which are other than those on which the particular right is founded, and which become strong enough to hold their own when a certain point is reached. . . . The boundary at which the conflicting interests balance cannot be determined by any general formula in advance, *but points in the line, or helping to establish it, are fixed by decisions that this or that concrete case falls on the nearer or farther side.*[11]

A decision, then, is never absolutely final, but rather, as Chief Justice Hughes said of dissenting opinions, ". . . an appeal to the brooding spirit of the law, to the intelligence of a future day"[12] when future decisions will perchance correct the error of the present one in the light of much discussion of the issues, more experience in living with the results, and, one hopes, of greater wisdom in the people. This system, if really working, would prevent the hardening of any and all particular forms. As Christians now speak of "religionless" Christianity, so one might say that the American system was designed to perpetuate "stateless" government.

To be sure the Supreme Court has declared in the Schempp-Murray decision that some points on the line have been "decisively settled":

> First, this Court has decisively settled that the First Amendment's mandate that "Congress shall make no law respecting an establishment of religion, or prohibiting the free exercise thereof" has been made wholly applicable to the states by the Fourteenth Amendment. . . . Second, this Court has rejected unequivocally the contention that the establishment clause forbids only governmental preference of one religion over another. . . . the Court said that "[n]either a state nor the Federal government can set up a church. Neither can pass laws which aid one religion, aid all religions, or prefer one religion over another." . . . "The [First] Amendment's purpose . . . was to create a complete and permanent separation of the spheres of religious activity and civil authority by comprehensively forbidding every form of public aid or support for religion."[13]

Perhaps this was merely a temporary lapse into undue optimism or into wishful thinking induced by fatigue.

I noted above that in the United States there is no "church" in the traditional institutional sense. What, then, is there? At most we may say that the catholic or universal church, the body of Christ, is here divided visibly into hundreds of institutions. It is important to have a clear idea of the nature of these institutions in the American system.

Madison's "sect," now commonly called a "church," is a tangible voluntary association for the pursuit of religious or spiritual ends. As "an ecclesiastical body . . . [it is] a law unto itself, [and] self-governing . . . in the discharge of its religious functions."[14] This means that the civil courts if called upon to adjudicate a conflict between factions within this body will do so on the basis of the polity of that particular body.[15]

But "an ecclesiastical body" as such has no recognized legal being. Its temporal interests are cared for and its responsibilities discharged by a corporation which is the creation of the civil authority and has recognized legal being. As such the corporation has justiciable rights and responsibilities. The corporation "is formed [primarily] for the acquisition and taking care of the property of the church, and is in no sense ecclesiastical [or spiritual] in its functions."[16] Because the ecclesiastical body can define the qualifications for membership in its corporation and censure or remove members for causes defined by its laws, the two are inextricably bound together.

Now then, when in Madison's words the civil authority in the interests of "preserving public order" protects a "sect" or church "against trespasses on its legal rights by others," the reference is to the corporation. This is why, as Supreme Court Justices have declared, it is not necessary for them in order to adjudicate conflicts between "sects" to understand or know what the particular "sects" involved, or scholars in general, mean by "religion." As Mr. Justice Jackson put it, the duty of the court "to apply the Bill of Rights to assertions of official authority" does not "depend upon our possession of marked competence in the field where the invasion of rights occurs."[17] They do not have to know what "religion" is in the abstract, to know when one sect, or group of sects, is infringing upon the rights of other sects, or of unbelievers, to "free exercise" and/or equal protection of the laws.

This is a point that religionists have sometimes greatly misunderstood. For example, in an article in *The Christian Century* of September 4, 1963, Clyde A. Holbrook argued that because scholars are not agreed on the "criteria for religious activity" the Supreme Court can have no "competence to distinguish religious acts from nonreligious acts" and therefore ought to "leave this area alone" at least "until such time as . . . [it] has done its homework on the nature of religion in American society."[18] Aside from the stop-the-world-we-want-to-get-off-for-the-time-being attitude implied by this stance, if Mr. Holbrook's position were imposed on the American situation it would mean that the civil authority would define for the "sects" what "religion" is—one of the precise things the founders with their knowledge of English Erastianism sought to avoid. As it is, the civil authority will protect the right of each "ecclesiastical body" to define "religion" as it chooses. And if, through its corporation, a "sect" attempts to trespass upon the similar right of other "sects" the civil courts may be appealed to, to prevent this.

Granted the traditional usage in Christendom, just as Jefferson's concept of the "church" conjures up the image of one monolithic ecclesiastical body in the society whose authority is vested in certain persons, so the concept of the "state" induces the image of one monolithic concentration of supreme civil authority vested in certain persons. But this image of the "state" is no more applicable to the American system than is that image of the "church." This nation never created such a "state." We should all be properly shocked if, reminiscent of Louis XIV, our elected national executive officers, senators, and congressmen should some day stand up in a body and declare, "We are the state!"

In the Anglo-American tradition since time immemorial an accepted premise has been that sovereignty resides in the people, and therefore government must be by the consent of the governed. In this context emerged the various forms of the myth of the contractual origins of society, of government, and of the state. Commonly there were three steps. In the first, individuals entered into reciprocal engagements with others to manage their common interests and secure their common happiness. This formed "society."

In the second step, having agreed to form society, they took measures to form the kind of government they wanted as the locus of supreme power in the commonwealth. In the third step this supreme power was vested in one or more persons. These persons, I take it, constituted "the state," or John Locke's "Legislative."

In one line of interpretation the people in these successive steps passed the sovereignty (supreme power) resident in them on to Locke's "Legislative." In this line Sir William Blackstone held that "Sovereignty and legislature are . . . convertible terms; one cannot subsist without the other." It followed in Blackstone's view, "the supreme and absolute authority of the state is vested . . . in the British Parliament." And "so long as the English constitution lasts" in which the people indicated their choice of government, "the power of parliament is absolute and without control" and what it does "no authority upon earth can undo."[19]

As I understand Locke's view, sovereignty is not thus completely and finally passed in this fashion to the legislative. In the second step the legislative is made "the *supream power* of the Commonwealth" and as such it is "sacred and unalterable in the hands where the Community have once placed it. . . . " But it is the *"supream power"* only in the sense that its edicts alone "have the force and obligation of a *Law*" of the Commonwealth.[20] But always "there remains still *in the people a Supream Power* to re-move or alter the *Legislative,* when they find the *Legislative* act contrary to the trust reposed in them. . . ."[21] This is a government of law, and it seems clear that sovereignty (the *"supream power"*) always remains in the people.

But Locke, in keeping with the English pattern, conceived the Legislative as "placed in the Concurrence of three distinct Persons," "An Assembly of Representatives chosen *pro tempore,* by the People," "An Assembly of Hereditary Nobility," and a hereditary monarch "having the constant, supream, executive Power, and with it the Power of Convoking and Dissolving the other two within certain Periods of Time."[22] When the Legislative or any part of it acts contrary to the trust reposed in it, they "put themselves into a state of War with the People, who are thereupon absolved from any further Obedience, and are left to the common Refuge, which God hath provided for all Men against Force and Violence,"[23] namely, contrary force. "For in all States and Conditions the true remedy of *Force* without Authority is to oppose Force to it. The use of *force* without Authority, always puts him that uses it into a *state of War,* as the Aggressor, and renders him liable to be treated accordingly."[24] It would appear, then, that to Locke, because there were hereditary elements in the Legislative, the *only* recourse of the people against tyranny on the part of the state was revolution.

The United States by eliminating hereditary elements from its Legislative, and (symbolically at least) completely returning *all* executive and legislative power to the people periodically in free elections, eliminated the elements most likely to become tyrannous because not subject to election. And these were the elements which, because of their permanency, carried the image of "the state" separate from the people. From Locke's point of view the American system might seem a government of continual and perpetual, albeit peaceful, revolution, in which the only possible tyranny was that of a majority. Hence the constitutional checks on the power of the majority, rooted primarily in the Bill of Rights.

This was the feature that so impressed Alexis de Tocqueville, who said that "any discussion of the political laws of the United States must always begin with the dogma of the sovereignty of the people." This principle, he continued, seems to be found "at the bottom of almost all human institutions" and it is commonly invoked and "abused [even] by intriguers and despots of every age." But usually, if publicly appealed to, "it is hastily thrust back into the gloom of the sanctuary"—that is, it is professed but not actualized in practice. However, Tocqueville argued, it was "the creative principle of most of the English colonies in America" exemplified in the practices of the townships. In the Revolution "the dogma of the sovereignty of the people came out from the township and took possession of the [national] government; every class enlisted in its cause; the war was fought and victory obtained in its name; it became the law of laws." Hence in the United States the principle "is neither hidden nor sterile as with some other nations; mores recognize it, and the laws proclaim it; it spreads with freedom and attains unimpeded its ultimate consequences." It swept away the traditional "voting qualifications," for once the principle was accepted, there was no "halting place until universal suffrage" was attained.

Consequently, in America, Tocqueville concluded, unlike most other countries, there is no "authority, in a sense outside the body social [which] influences it and forces it to progress in a certain direction" (e.g., a church), and not even a divided power which is "at the same time within the society and outside it" (e.g., a hereditary monarch and/or lords). For in the United States

society acts by and for itself. There are no authorities except within itself; one can hardly meet anybody who would dare to conceive, much less to suggest, seeking power elsewhere. The people take part in the making of the laws by choosing the lawgivers, and they share in their application by electing the agents of the executive power; one might say that they govern themselves, so feeble and restricted is the part left to the administration, so vividly is that administration aware of its popular origin, and so obedient is it to the fount of power. The people reign over the American political world as God rules over the universe. It is the cause and the end of all things; everything rises out of it and is absorbed back into it.[25]

In this context regular elections on all levels symbolize the continual return of sovereignty to the people who in Locke's phrase "shall be judge" of whether or not their representatives are fulfilling the trust temporarily placed in them. Seen in this perspective, our constitutional federalism and all the elaborate mechanisms or procedures observed in the practice of our Republic are merely means devised to actualize government by the immediate consent of the governed. There is no "state" in the traditional sense.

In 1837 Senator Asher Robbins of Rhode Island interpreted James Madison's vision very much in Tocqueville's terms. It was, he said, that "this scattered and countless multitude were to be ruled in freedom as one people and by the popular will—that will was to be uncontrolled in itself, and controlling everything." Robbins thought that Madison realized that "such an achievement the most enlightened friends of freedom and human rights, in all countries, and in all ages, had deemed to be morally and physically impossible." In the face of this almost universal negative, the task confronted by Madison and his co-workers was to institute "one simple [overall] government, with all the purposes of peace and war" without completely absorbing and thus destroying "as States" the original "thirteen States, and all the other States to be formed out of that vast territory. . . ." Here the traditional concept of the unitary state, if clung to, would make the job impossible by definition, and the alternative of a confederation of sovereign states had already been tried and found wanting. Senator Robbins located Madison's and the Americans' genius, first, in their concept of "federalism"—a novel principle "unexplored and unknown before . . . our confederate and national republic"; and, second, in the astute political ability they displayed "in engineering this system from idea to reality."[26]

It seems, then, that the Americans departed from Locke in this very important respect. To Locke, apparently, sovereignty was indivisible, and he could not conceive of distributing the sovereignty resident in the people between several "legislatives."[27] He held that "there can be but *one Supream Power,* which is the *Legislative,* to which all the rest are and must be subordinate. . . ."[28] This, I suppose, is the common conception of the unitary "state."

The Americans created, not this, but a federalism which in Felix Frankfurter's words "presupposes the distribution of governmental powers between national and local authority. Between these two authorities there is shared the power entirely possessed by a unitary state."[29] This means that there could be no American "state" in the traditional sense. And the situation is further complicated by the fact that "In addition to the provisions of our Constitution making this distribution of authority between the two governments, there is also in the United States Constitution a withdrawal of power from both governments, or, at least, the exercise of governmental power is subject to limitations protective of the rights of the individual."[30] Because and insofar as the areas of authority of the national and local governments are defined, the latter are not "subordinate" in Locke's sense to the former. Each is in its defined area a locus of the supreme power. In addition, the individual has both enumerated (the Bill of Rights) and unenumerated (Ninth Amendment) rights, recognition of which limits the power of both national and local authorities.

In this situation "the Supreme Court," as Mr. Justice Brennan put it, "has been assigned the unique responsibility for umpiring our federal system."[31] Its work was described by Mr. Justice Jackson as that of "arbitrating the allocation of powers between different branches of the Federal Government, between state and nation, between state and state, and between majority government and minority rights."[32]

Once one grasps the tremendous complexity of the possible relationships between the hundreds of religious bodies and between one or more of them and one or more of the many institutionalized foci of the civil authority, he sees the complete inadequacy of Jefferson's simple concepts of a wall, a church, and a state to encompass and promote understanding of the actualities of the American situation. In America both the "church," as such, and the "state" in the traditional sense are conceptual abstractions not applicable to the realities experienced in the United States.

Even the Supreme Court cannot adjudicate differences between two abstractions, at least not when the names for them are not found in the Constitution, which it is the Justices' job to interpret. It can only adjudicate practical differences between entities in the society with legal being and standing. It is specifically precluded from "rendering . . . every form of pronouncement on abstract, contingent, or hypothetical issues."[33] This is why if we think with Jefferson's concepts of "church" and "state" we tend not to discuss the actual problems and legal issues before us but, rather, the differences between two abstractions which can be dealt with only hypothetically and resolved only in the realm of ideas. It is this that seems to me to give an air of unreality to many of the discussions of "church and state" in the United States and serves to distract attention from notice and discussion of one of the chief sources of conflicts over matters pertaining to religion, namely, the clashes between the religious "sects" themselves.

We should be mindful of the fact that from the viewpoint of those responsible for the civil order in the nations of Christendom during the past four hundred years, "religion" organized in many "sects" has not been a unifying force but a divisive element in the body politic. And the clashes between the religious "sects" are periodically still threats to "the domestic tranquility" if not to the political society itself.

For centuries some ecclesiastical bodies were armed, either directly or indirectly, with coercive power in the defense of their "orthodox" beliefs and practices. And they often used every weapon in the arsenal of physical violence against the heretic, dissenter, or schismatic person. It was the civil authority that deprived them of these weapons. If we now admit that Christians were wrong in using such weapons in defense of the gospel of Jesus Christ, it seems to me that credit is due the religiously "neutral" civil authority that took the Sword of Steel from them and left them dependent upon the Sword of the Spirit alone. If our theology permits, we may even suppose that God was using the civil authority to force Christians to act overtly in accordance with what they professed. And this might suggest an area in which to begin to look for a theological justification of our form of civil government. But instead of probing in this direction, some religionists continue to speak pejoratively of the "secular" or "godless" state.

Madison's "sects" are the only religious institutions that have legal being, rights, and standing in the United States. Their corporate differences can, and often have, resulted in justiciable issues subject to adjudication in the civil courts and having far-reaching consequences. For example, the progressive elimination of religious exercises in the public schools in the forms of Bible reading and prayers was not the result of initiative on the part of the civil authorities, but rather, the result of the initiative of religious groups that rightly questioned the legality of using the civil power to impose the forms of a particular "sect" or group of "sects" on all the persons in a public institution of the pluralistic society.[34]

The civil authorities, indeed, have little opportunity to take the initiative in religious matters. Acceptance of the idea of a commonwealth with religious pluralism and conflicting "ecclesiastical bodies" forced the civil authority to assume an attitude of neutrality toward their conflicting claims, neither helping nor hindering any religious institution, while protecting the rights of each and all. For when all the religious groups are equal before the law, the authority which must adjudicate the differences between them that threaten the civil order cannot be a party in the conflicts—as was the case in Christendom for centuries.

Of course, it may be assumed that the civil authorities in adjudicating the differences between "ecclesiastical bodies" must have some guidelines, presumably rooted in some conception of the nature of man and his relation to the cosmos in which he finds himself. The philosophical and/or theological context implied here I call "the religion of the Republic." What is it? I find it at least adumbrated in the "enlightened" thought of the eighteenth century and the Protestant evangelical thought of the nineteenth. I have argued, therefore, that the heart of the matter for religionists is not, in any traditional sense, an issue between "church" and "state," but the theological issue between the particularistic theologies of the "sects" and the cosmopolitan theology of the Republic. But I cannot claim competence in this area, and wish that more of our professional theologians would take up the question.

6

Religion, Constitutional Federalism, Rights, and the Court[1]

The legal profession in all countries knows that there are only two real choices of government open to a people. It may be governed by law or it may be governed by the will of one or a group of men. Law, as the expression of the ultimate will and wisdom of a people, has so far proven the safest guardian of liberty yet devised.[2]

Our nation is pluralistic by inheritance and nature. The United States, wrote Philip Schaff in 1855, presents "a motley sampler of all church history, and the results it has thus far attained."[3] During the century since Schaff wrote, to all the Christian denominations and sects that he noted have been added organized representatives of all the world's religions plus a few religions invented here. Each is an interest group competing with all the others.

Granted this multiplicity of competing religious groups there are bound to be disputes and conflicts that threaten the civil order. How one thinks such conflicts ought to be settled depends upon his understanding of the nature of the democratic republic and especially of the role of the law and the courts in it. It has seemed to me that many attempts to discuss a church-state issue in the

United States reveal a lack of such understanding.[4] This essay attempts only an elementary "map" of the system.

There are many definitions of "democracy." We may begin with that of Judge Learned Hand: "Democracy is a political contrivance by which the group conflicts inevitable in all society should find a relatively harmless outlet in the give and take of legislative compromise." This means that democratic government is a method— a means to an end, and not an end in itself. The end, in general terms, is the securing of "life, liberty, and the pursuit of happiness."

In this context, as Professor Harry Jones noted, ". . . it is law's unique role in a democratic society to accomplish a resolution, at least a tolerable accommodation, of the conflicting interests and opposed demands that are inevitable in any dynamic community."[5] The point is that in a pluralistic society such as ours compromise and accommodation of absolutistic claims in practice are of the essence. If it is working no individual, no group, no faction, no interest can have his or its way completely. Every group must learn to live with less than the whole pie precisely in order that the others may live also in their way with their due part. This is difficult for the religious groups, not only because religious commitment is an all-or-nothing stance, but also because most of the old-line denominations grew up in national households like spoiled only children, each accustomed to having its way while being fed, clothed, and protected from interference by a civil power. The attitudes developed during such upbringing are hard to eradicate, and the persistence of "sectarianism"[6] is evidence that they still exist in the religious groups.

But the law plays not only the negative role of preserving the general welfare and outward peace. It also plays a positive role in forming, shaping, and consolidating what Adolf Berle called the "public consensus"[7] that binds society together. Laws may "encourage the virtuous" as well as "restrain the vicious."[8]

The law, for example, may induce some reluctant Christians to live up to their Master's command. For, if Matthew 5:44[9] be interpreted as a command to every sect as well as to individual Christians, then the civil law that forbids a sect to retaliate overtly against those who curse or despitefully use it plays a positive role in restraining Christians to act as if they were exhibiting the charity they profess. There is little evidence that they exercised such charity until the authority of a commonwealth constrained them to do so.[10] To civil authority the religious groups had become divisive and destructive. It could no longer maintain religious uniformity. Therefore it had to try to maintain peace and order between the sects, and in order to do so it had to become neutral so far as the sects' particularistic claims were concerned.

It may be admitted that charity and forbearance cannot be legislated. But overt action reflecting its absence may be controlled by positive law. As Martin Luther King, Jr., put it, "A law can't force a man to love me, but it can keep him from lynching me. A law can't change the heart but it can restrain the heartless."[11] We too readily forget that at least from the time of the Toleration Act in Maryland in 1649 the outward appearance of the exercise of such charity and forbearance was again and again forced upon religious sectarians in the English colonies by law or authoritative decree.

1. FEDERALISM

Now let us look at the constitutional federalism under which all the denominations live in the United States—and at its legal structure which was set up, negatively, to resolve conflicts, adjudicate differences, and accomplish tolerable accommodations in the commonwealth, and, positively, "to form a more perfect Union, establish Justice, insure domestic Tranquility, provide for the common defense, promote the general Welfare, and secure the blessings of Liberty to ourselves and our Posterity."

"Government" refers to the institution(s) accepted as the sole wielder(s) of coercive power—the locus (or loci) of legitimated authority—in the society. It is a truism that "the Government can suffer no rivals in the field of coercion."[12] The government of the United States is a federalism, in which governmental powers are not concentrated in a unitary state, but are distributed between national and local authorities, each of which, in its defined realm, is an institutionalized locus of the supreme sovereignty.[13]

In addition "the exercise of governmental power [by either or both] is subject to limitations protective of the rights of the individual."[14] It is obvious that the distribution of power between the national and local authorities is bound to lead to conflicts requiring adjudication. It is equally obvious that restrictions on the authority of both over the individual citizen are similarly bound to lead to conflicts. For in the nature of things, as Justice William J. Brennan put it, ". . . no genius of constitution making could have delineated the precise boundaries of the powers assigned the several repositories of governmental power . . . [or] fashioned precise guidelines for the resolution of the myriad collisions between power exercised by any of these repositories and the guarantees of individual liberty erected to restrain governmental oppression whatever its source." In this situation "some institution had to referee these conflicts, and the Framers chose the Supreme Court ultimately to perform that duty"—an extremely difficult duty because necessarily "the guide lines are indistinct."[15]

But the guidelines are there, "in the Constitution"—which

phrase I put in quotation marks to remind us again that what is "in" the Constitution is in practice something that the Supreme Court decides. In other words, for the time being at least, the Constitution means in any particular justiciable issue what the majority of the court says it means. To understand this, one must see it in the context of the inclusive meaning and implications of government under a written Constitution.

2. CONSTITUTIONALISM

Constitutionalism means government by defined law rather than by "one [man] or a group of men." A written constitution is, first of all, a statement of the fundamental principles of a body politic that defines the locus of the sovereign power (e.g., in "the people"); its distribution (e.g., federalism); the structure of the government and the relation between the parts (e.g., legislative, executive, and judicial). Second, it is a statement of the rules governing the forming and perpetuation of the government (e.g., for adopting the Constitution, eligibility for office, elections); for adjudicating differences that arise within the body; and amending the Constitution itself. Necessarily the principles have to be stated on a level of high generality, the rules somewhat less so. Together they constitute the guidelines, and their indistinctness is commensurate with their generality. That is why umpires or referees are necessary, namely, to decide what a particular generality in the Constitution means when applied to a specific controverted point. To ask if something is "constitutional" is to ask if it is consistent with the fundamental principles of the nation. In this sense the court functions as the guardian of the character of the Republic.

By the time the English colonies were firmly planted on the eastern seaboard of America, the ideas were well established that "the power of the ruler should be exercised in accordance with established fundamental law, and that the government should owe its existence to a compact of the governed."[16] Thomas Hooker, preaching at Hartford, Connecticut in 1638, insisted that "the foundation of authority is laid, firstly, in the free consent of the people."[17] And ten years later in his *A Survey of the Summe of Church Discipline* he argued that before a person has any power over another "there must of necessity be a mutuall ingagement, each of the other, by their free consent, before by any rule of God they have any right or power or can exercise either, each towards the other."[18]

The concept of the consent of the governed was rooted in the image of men in the "state of nature" wherein no person had any right of power over another. Because it is questionable that any thinker really supposed either that such a state had actually existed or that such a contract was a historical reality,[19] we may call this a myth. But it was a myth of tremendous motivational power during the seventeenth and eighteenth centuries in overthrowing old governments and establishing new forms.

The concept reflected the great conceptual revolution that inverted the traditional view of the flow of God's power for the creation of ordered communities. Traditionally the image had been of the flow of such power from the top down through a man or a group of men thought of as divine or peculiarly accessible to Deity. Now the image became that of the flow of such power from the bottom up—from and through "the people" to rulers chosen by them. "God," said John Locke, "who hath given the World to Men in common, hath also given them reason to make use of it to the best advantage of Life and convenience."[20] In this view, the law no longer originates on some mountaintop above the clouds to be brought down to the people by some God-ordained

Moses. Rather, the power of God for the formation of law is *in* "the people," and "Moses" becomes their elected deputy.

Government, it follows, is an instrument which men create by reason and choice because they see its advantages as well as its necessity. Conceptually all power is from God, and God ordains government. But now the power on earth is resident first in "the people," and rulers have power only as a "trust reposed in them" by "the people." It follows that such rulers must "govern by *declared* and *received Laws,* and not by extemporary Dictates and undetermined Resolutions."[21] And *"The People shall be Judge"* of whether or not their chosen legislators "act contrary to their Trust."[22] Hence, so far as the creation of ordered communities is concerned, the people might be said to be enjoined in the words of Philippians 2:12–13: ". . . work out your own salvation with fear and trembling. For it is God which worketh in you both to will and to do of his good pleasure."[23]

The myth, then, is that the people institute government by entering into a covenant (compact, contract) with one another, primarily to secure their rights. The Constitution lays down the terms of the contract—the rule of conduct to be observed and followed—the "guidelines," adherence to which is deemed most efficacious in protecting the individual's rights while promoting and defending the general welfare. One *consents* to these terms of the contract, which implies that he accepts certain responsibilities and duties that, within defined limits, he can be coerced to assume.

But because the ultimate sovereign power *on earth* is in "the people" and the government is their instrument, the Constitution itself provides that the people may alter the fundamental law and, as part of the contract, lays down the rules to be followed in amending it. But the people also reserve the radical right when "any form of Government becomes destructive of these ends . . .

to abolish it, and to institute new Government" deemed more likely to achieve their ends. Abraham Lincoln in his First Inaugural Address summarized these principles in classic style: "This country, with its institutions, belongs to the people who inhabit it. Whenever they shall grow weary of the existing Government, they can exercise their constitutional right of amending it or their revolutionary right to dismember or overthrow it."[24]

Constitutionalism plus religious pluralism forced the "secularization" of government—for "secularization" means the "de-sectarianization" of government, that is, the civil authority must become neutral where the particularistic claims of the sects are concerned.[25] For government is for *all* men in society, and *all* men enter into the compact that forms it. As Judge H. M. Brackenridge put it in 1819 in protesting the Maryland law excluding Jews from public office, "our political compacts are not entered into as brethren of the Christian faith—but as men, as members of a civilized society."[26]

Implicit here is the conception of appeal to a universal principle that transcends not only the particularities that distinguish the Christian denominations or sects from one another, but also the particularities that distinguish one world religion from another. "*All* men are created equal," of whatever religion, denomination, or sect whatsoever, and all are equally endowed "with certain unalienable rights."[27]

It is helpful to think of American constitutional government as a game which "we the people" have engaged to play for the high stakes of freedom. The game has defined and known rules that are consented to as a condition of entering the game. The rules define the nature of the game, and set limits to permissible conduct in playing it. Referees or umpires are recognized as having power to interpret the rule-book of the game, and their decisions have the sanction of coercive power if necessary. The rules themselves include a provision for modifying them without changing the basic character of the game (the constitutional right to amend). And, of course, it is recognized that the players also have the right, if they grow weary of the game, to change to another game with a different set of rules (the revolutionary right). Therefore it is very important if and when we question the decisions of the recognized referees to be very clear whether we are merely advocating amending the existing rules, or whether we are advocating shifting to a different kind of game. When uncomfortable or outraged with Supreme Court decisions striking down the Regents' prayer or Bible reading and recitation of the Lord's Prayer in the schools, people advocated the Becker, Dirksen, or similar amendments, they were playing the game according to the rules. But if, as reported in the papers, a speaker in southern California declared that the Chief Justice ought to be hanged because of a decision the court made, he was advocating that we change to another kind of game.

3. RIGHTS

The concept of unalienable rights of the individual citizen was the corollary of constitutionalism. Anciently the power of God for the creation of ordered human communities, conceived primarily as coercive, was channeled through specially designated *powers* on earth—a priest-king or an elite—who wielded it to create ordered communities. Rather early in Christendom even the power of God for salvation (grace) came under the monopolistic control of a self-perpetuating line of priests (the "church") through whom alone grace was made available to ordinary mortals. With the emergence of the nations a particular church became coextensive with a state.[28] The Reformation's "right-wing" churches were the tribal cults of the new nations.

The individual as a citizen-church member had no inherent rights that he could assert against the supposedly ordained repositories of power. He had, it was argued, "no other Remedy but Patience" for "that an Inferiour should punish a Superiour, is against Nature."[29] That the people must not defend themselves even against a "King imperiously domineering over them"[30] was sometimes deduced from Romans 13:1-2: ". . . there is no power but of God; and they that withstand shall receive to themselves judgment." Resistance was a sin as well as a civil offense. To be sure, the hard lot of the individual under the laws civil-ecclesiastical might be alleviated by monarch or priest. But such alleviation was an act of grace—a sheer gift. Some gifts of grace might become habitual in a society as "privileges" customarily granted by "the *powers*" but subject to withdrawal at their whim. We should not confuse such "privileges" with "rights."

The conceptual revolution noted above inverted this order, placing the power of God for the forming of communities in the people, making all rulers their deputies. And "the *Fundamental Law* of [their] Nature," said Locke, "being *the preservation of Mankind,* no Humane Sanction can be good or valid against it."[31] Therefore the basic collective right of the people is self-defense against outside enemies *or* their own chosen rulers who may become derelict in their duties. This, said Locke, is "the common Refuge which God hath provided for all Men against Force and Violence."[32]

The concept of government by consent of the governed implies that some rights are reserved by the individual—"every Man has a *Property* in his own *Person.* This no Body has any Right to but himself."[33] The obverse side of a right is a duty. An "unalienable" right is one that a person cannot relinquish the responsibility for exercising even if he thinks he wants to. "The care of every man's soul belongs to himself," Jefferson said. "The magistrate has no power but what the people gave," and they "have not given him the care of souls because they could not; they could not, because no man has *right* to abandon the care of his salvation to another."[34]

As noted above, in defining "federalism," the conception of rights operates as a limitation on the exercise of both national and local governmental authority over the individual. It is important that we understand why this is so.

In the practice of constitutionalism all the major decisions are reached through majority vote. But it is a majority operating under defined law. Part of that fundamental law is the Bill of Rights that limits "the power of the majority [even when] duly expressed through governmental action."[35] As Mr. Justice Robert H. Jackson summarized in the Barnette case (1943):

> The very purpose of a Bill of Rights was to withdraw certain subjects from the vicissitudes of political controversy, to place them beyond the reach of majorities and officials and to establish them as legal principles to be applied by the courts. One's right to life, liberty, and property, to free speech, a free press, freedom of worship and assembly, and other fundamental rights may not be submitted to vote; they depend on the outcome of no elections.[36]

Where religion is concerned, the Bill of Rights exists to protect minorities against "the tyranny of a majority" after long experience had shown "that society cannot trust the conscience of a majority to keep its religious zeal within the limits that a free society can tolerate."[37] This has important bearing on the permission of religious exercises in the public schools. The forms of worship would presumably be determined by majority vote—local, state, or national. Therefore, the proper question to ask is not, "Would you approve of prayers and/or Bible reading in the public schools?" but rather, "Would you as a member of a minority religious group (and in the United States every religious group is a minority) want the majority given the power to impose its form of worship on all the children in the schools?"

While a Bill of Rights may be part of the fundamental law of a nation, "it is the first axiom of a constitutional government that declarations of rights are meaningless, or can be made so, if there are no remedies to enforce them." And in the constitutionalism of the United States "that remedy is provided . . . by the power of the courts, the ordinary courts, to review the constitutionality of legislative and executive action, and, if it violates constitutional principles, declare it void and ineffective."[38]

In other words, the Constitution enumerates only *some* of the rights of a citizen. The Ninth Amendment reminds us that there are other rights not listed. The principle of judicial review means that the citizen can appeal to the courts if and when he thinks a right is being infringed by any legislative or executive action. In this sense the courts are the protectors of the citizen against legislative or executive infringement of his rights. The Supreme Court, in interpreting what the Constitution means, speaks for "the people"—the Constitution being the symbol of the sovereignty of the people. Or, as summarized by Justice Jackson in his Barnette case opinion, "the Fourteenth Amendment, as now applied to the states, protects the citizen against the State itself and all its creatures—Boards of Education not excepted."[39]

It is important to understand the nature and purpose of the Bill of Rights and how its provisions are enforced. Well-meaning people, who apparently did not understand its implications, have argued that striking down a state or local law requiring religious exercises in its public schools, which law was enacted "with the consent of the majority of those affected, collides with the majority's right of free exercise of religion." Rightly Justice Tom Clark replied that "while the Free Exercise Clause clearly prohibits the use of state action to deny the rights of free exercise to *anyone,* it has never meant that a majority could use the machinery of the State to practice its beliefs,"[40] and compel observance of its *religious* exercises by all. This would be to deny free exercise to all the minorities.

4. THE SUPREME COURT

The Constitution is the rule-book of the game we are playing. But the game is so vast and so complex that the rules of necessity must be broad and inclusive. As Lincoln put it: ". . . no organic law can ever be framed with a provision specifically applicable to every question which may occur in practical administration. No foresight can anticipate nor any document of reasonable length contain express provisions for all possible questions."[41]

The provisions in the Bill of Rights have the form of abstract general principles. It is the duty of the Justices in every case to determine what these universal principles mean when applied to the specific issue before them. Obviously there are many points on which able and reasonable men may disagree. Hence the frequency of divisions in the Supreme Court. Thus through a process of "constitutional exegesis"[42] the court performs its awesome task of "arbitrating the allocation of powers between different branches of the Federal Government, between state and nation, between state and state, and between majority government and minority rights."[43]

Yet in spite of its great responsibility, the court is a peculiar and rather fragile institution in the American system. On the one hand it has status as an independent unit of government. But it is "in vital respects a dependent body,"[44] its makeup, powers, and limitations ambiguously defined in the Constitution (Article III), and its most visible aspect, appellate jurisdiction, the creation of Congress in the Judiciary Act of 1789.[45] Its most impressive power is that of judicial review of the constitutionality of legislative or executive acts. But this power "is not expressly granted or hinted at in the Article defining judicial power, but rests on logical implication."[46] It is for this reason that "[John] Marshall's great constitutional decisions" establishing this power "cite no precedents. . . . they are argued out of political philosophy. . . ."[47]

Because it is a court it is "a substantially passive instrument" of government that can be "moved only by the initiative of litigants."[48] This means that the court cannot go out looking for controverted issues to be resolved. It follows that the issues brought to it closely reflect the primary areas of political conflict in the society at the time.[49] Further, to make the appellate work of the court manageable, "Congress has found it necessary to make review in the Supreme Court not the right of the litigant but a discretionary matter with the Court itself."[50] In a typical year only 119 of 1,452 cases presented were allowed. Naturally there is a tendency to select those cases that present very pressing issues. It is for these reasons that "the Constitution has gone through several cycles of interpretation" during the years, each cycle of emphasis reflecting the "political and economic condition of the period."[51] Therefore it should be kept in mind that "when judges do not agree, it is a sign that they are dealing with problems on which society itself is divided."[52]

Perhaps the greatest limitation on the court, and the one least understood, is that its judicial power "extends only to cases and controversies."[53] It has "but one function—that of deciding litigations. . . ."[54] This means that it cannot act unless an occasion to act is brought to it. Yet, in spite of all these ambiguities and limitations, the court has thus far rather successfully operated in our system to "accomplish a resolution, [or] at least a tolerable accommodation" of the innumerable "conflicting interests and opposed demands" of the pluralistic nation. In other words, it has been the chief instrument for the maintenance of a government of law.[55]

The Supreme Court is a court is a court—on this we must be clear. It is not a philosophical club, not a debating society, not an academic discussion group that meets to discuss and define the ideal, abstract, and theological meanings of such terms as "religious freedom," "separation," "establishment," "free exercise," and so on. In fact it is precluded from "rendering . . . every form of pronouncement on abstract, contingent, or hypothetical issues."[56]

Because the court *is* a court the Justices "have to adjudicate" within a time limit. Once they have taken a case they have to publish a decision with all its multifarious implications and in the midst of all the ambiguities of the contending claims that usually involve the legitimate invocations of "more than one so-called principle."[57]

In the words of Mr. Justice Felix Frankfurter, "If the conflict cannot be resolved, the task of the Court is to arrive at an accommodation of the contending claims. This is the core of the difficulties and misunderstandings about the judicial process."[58] This is the agony induced by the necessity to come to a definite decision in the midst of ambiguity, while knowing that the decision will have far-reaching consequences in the lives of human beings. In the context of the idea that the court is the guardian of the character of the Republic its decisions are moral decisions. And the consequences of a moral decision of this kind cannot be known in advance.

Finally, the court has no coercive power at its command, and is completely "dependent upon the political branches for the execution of its mandates." Every schoolboy learns that President Jackson once withheld enforcement, saying, " 'John Marshall has made his decision: now let him enforce it!' "[59]

Here one can see the plausibility of Robert G. McCloskey's conclusion (a disputed interpretation to be sure) that Congress can "decide whether the Supreme Court will be a significant or a peripheral factor in American government."[60] For as the then emeritus Justice Owen J. Roberts put it, probably there is nothing but tradition to prevent Congress from taking away "all the appellate jurisdiction of the Supreme Court . . ." because Congress defines "in what cases the Supreme Court can entertain an appeal."[61] Because judicial review alone places limits on the legislative power, to strip the court of this power would have the effect of making the legislative power supreme with the judicial power subservient to it.[62] This, so long as the outward forms of the Republic prevailed, would in effect make a majority supreme, and against it minorities would have no appeal. This is why eternal vigilance in support of freedom in the pluralistic society entails a perpetual "fuss over the rights of minorities" which well-meaning citizens have railed against.[63]

And "the people shall be judge" of what they want, and deserve what they get. For the whole system rests on the public consensus. Thus far, as Mr. Justice Jackson noted, public opinion has seemed "always to sustain the power of the Court, even against attack by popular executives and even though the public more than once has repudiated particular decisions."[64] This is to say that the people thus far have indicated that this is the game that they want to play for the high stakes of freedom, and they have been willing to stick to the rules of the game. "The people have seemed to feel that the Supreme Court, whatever its defects, is still the most detached, dispassionate, and trustworthy custodian that our system affords for the translation of abstract into concrete constitutional commands."[65]

It is clear that the whole system of constitutional federalism rests on the belief that the Constitution as interpreted by the Supreme Court is the highest authority of the nation for the resolution of conflicts in the society. I see no way to "prove" this. All one can do is point to the "fact" that this is the case. "Civil liberties had their origin and must find their ultimate guaranty in the faith of the people."[66] In practice this means their faith that the application of the principles laid down in the Constitution is the surest defense of their rights and freedoms.

Perhaps there is a lesson to be learned by thinking analogically of what happened to the visible church in Christendom when enough people ceased to believe that the Bible *as interpreted by the ecclesiastical institution* was the highest authority for the guidance of their lives. For when they rejected the institution's authority to interpret the concrete meaning of the Bible's principles for all, and insisted upon "no rule but the Scriptures" *and* the "right of private judgment" in its interpretation, the visible universal church was fragmented into mutually murderous warring sects, and, as some predicted, belief in the Bible as highest authority followed apace.[67] When in the society there was no longer an agreed upon institutionalized locus for the adjudication of differences between members of the Christian household of faith, the centripetal force of a common authority was overcome by the centrifugal force of individual freedom and the *catholic* church flew apart. I think that an analogous situation would follow in the nation if every minority began to insist on the "right of private judgment" in interpreting the Constitution. Then as the consequent threat of anarchy and chaos was widely observed, we would expect some form of tyrannical control in the name of law and order for the preservation of outward unity in the face of enemies from without. As Lincoln said, a people have just three possibilities in government—anarchy (which is no-government), despotism, and consent (now called participatory authority).

At present, fragmentation seems a less obvious threat than centralization—the tendency "to move the center of gravity from the state capital to that of the nation."[68] This tendency is understandable and justifiable enough in the context of technological development that, as Adlai Stevenson said, has made counties out of continents and lakes out of oceans. Nevertheless, the threat to individual freedom inherent in the workings of vast national bureaucracies is clear enough to make them a legitimate object of attack. But we must note that such necessary attack can take forms that tend to undermine the prevailing consensus that the Constitution *as interpreted by the Supreme Court* is the highest authority for the resolution of conflicts within the commonwealth.

The saving factor in the situation is that the Constitution is a flexible instrument, "designed for a developing nation." It delineates, as Mr. Justice Frankfurter put it, "the skeleton or framework of our society—the anatomical as against the physiological aspects."[69] Continued growth is possible because "those features of our Constitution which raise the most frequent perplexities for a decision by the Court . . . were drawn in many particulars with purposeful vagueness so as to leave room for the unfolding but undisclosed future."[70]

In summary, as Mr. Justice Jackson said, ". . . the destiny of this Court is inseparably linked to the fate of our democratic system of government, . . ."[71] and the fate of our democratic system hinges upon the vision and faith of the people. As the ancient wisdom had it, where there is no vision the people perish, so it might now be said that not only the just, but also the free, must live by faith.

7

Religion of (or and) the Republic[1]

In February 1964 I made my first public appearance at the University of Iowa in a Humanities Society lecture entitled "Aspects of the Church-State Question." Since then much academic water has flowed over my intellectual bridges and under my academic damns and I have learned the hard way that there are more "Aspects of the Church-State Question" than I had dreamed of then. For ingenious (or do I mean "ingenuous"?) minds, sharpened on academic grindstones and propelled by the publications bogey, have cut so many capers about the topic as to envelop it in a thick verbal dust trailing clouds of impeccable footnotes.

Under the circumstances, it is manifestly impossible to speak with equal intelligibility to every hearer. Some are familiar with the points and counterpoints of a discussion fast bordering on a fracas, others have only a peripheral interest in it, and a few come along only for the ride. Because the subject is "religion," a majority probably have their minds unalterably made up. For "religion" is one area in which even some intellectuals seem to think themselves gifted with direct, immediate, intuited definitions and insights, from which they sometimes pontificate that it is no proper subject for university perusal.

Naturally, a great deal of the discussion of the religion of the Republic has swirled about the definition of "religion." Here it is important to note that in our pluralistic and competitive society "religion" is experienced and hence defined from two quite different perspectives—from that of an insider, and from that of an outsider. Because religious commitment is an all-or-nothing business, what the insider says about his denomination and *the* church is analogous to autobiography. During the centuries of Christianity, extremely able theologians have explained to the faithful, if not to the satisfaction of the unbeliever, why a person uninitiated by saving grace cannot possibly understand what it is all about. Jonathan Edwards directed one of the great minds of the ages to expounding the conclusion that the unregenerate outsider could not understand his (Edwards's) religious experience any more than the person with no sense of taste could comprehend the sweet taste of honey. One who had no sense of taste at all, of course, could not even have an analogical notion of what honey tastes like. Thus, most Christians seem to me to live comfortably within the aura of an assumed common experience, usually unaware that their ancestors, by pouring that experience into an institutional mold, created for their offspring a protective shell impervious to attack from the outside. The box turtle, when he pulls in his head, may rightly claim that you cannot know what goes on inside his shell.

From the perspective of those who have and do live outside religion's temple, or shell, a notion of what "religion" is must be a conclusion drawn from an analysis of what self-styled "religious" people do, in person and in institutions. In other words, the outsider can produce only a biography of "religion."

But now, in our pluralistic societies since the eighteenth century, the word "religion" points to a genus in which there are thousands of different species, each with its own peculiar protective institutional shell. The Yearbooks of the churches commonly list about 350 organized religious groups in the United States, and an able student of such matters has told me that he can come up with at least seven hundred that are unlisted. Members of each of these groups are prone to invoke, implicitly at least, the autobiography-biography analogy in defense of their "religion," against not only the un- or ir- or non-religious, but against all other "religions" falsely so-called. Hence the popularity of the pejorative references to "fringe" group, "pseudo" religion, and "sect" that some insiders use to point to those beyond their particular pale. These terms seem to be not so much categories invoked to distinguish the right and/or proper from the wrong and/or improper, as useful reminders of the snobbishness lingering in those who have little left to be snobbish about.

But the many species of the genus "religion" not only encounter each other in a highly competitive market; each and every one of them also encounters, one way or another, civil authority. And civil authority in our federalist system has many locuses—upward of eight thousand I have been told. With at least one thousand organized religious groups, and eight thousand centers of civil authority, the intricacy of possible relations between them, and the innumerable possibilities of collision, are obvious. Granted this situation, and in Pogo's phrase, it is to wonder at the persistence of formulating the relation in the pre-eighteenth-century categories of "church" and "state," as if we were still discussing the relatively simple relation between two recognized authorities in the commonwealth—*the* church and *the* state.

The inadequacy of these terms when applied to the situation in the United States, and the confusion that results from doing so, are commonly recognized today, even by some who continue to use them.

My primary interest in this discussion is not what religion *is,* but what it *does.* From my perspective, the definition of what religion is, is a matter for sectarian insiders to quarrel about—as they always have done, are now doing, and no doubt shall continue to do. I think the method of the outsider must be functional; that his ideal purpose is to delineate the effect religious beliefs and convictions have had upon what people did and the way they did it.[2] One explains what people did and why they did it by pointing to their motives. The study of "religion in American History" is the study, for example, of how religious convictions were incarnated in movements and in institutions: the Commonwealth of Massachusetts Bay, the Church of Jesus Christ of Latter-day Saints, the Seventh-day Adventist Church, Jane Addams's Hull House, or the Republic itself.[3]

My interest in the area that I have called, now somewhat to my regret, the religion of the Republic, was sparked during the era of the "post-Protestant" fad among the jet-set theologians during the first part of the 1960s. It seemed to me then that the post-Protestant faddists, insiders all, were compounding several errors: that confrontation with religious pluralism was a new thing in America; that the concept of religion (or Christianity) "in general" was a twentieth-century emergent; and that the constitutional and legal structures of the United States were once particularistically Protestant. All of these notions seemed to me to ignore the constellation of ideas that dominated the thinking of those we call the nation's founders.[4] That constellation seemed to me, and still seems, rightfully called "religious," if for no other reason than that its primary presupposition was the existence of the Deity, who had created the world and who governed it by his providence. These things Benjamin Franklin asserted he never doubted. Learned insiders from Timothy Dwight to Winthrop Hudson have proclaimed the obvious, that this constellation of ideas is not "distinctively Christian,"[5] and have tended, with the innocent aplomb of Fielding's Parson Thwackum, to assert or imply that therefore it was not "religious" at all.

Against that conclusion I want to assert with Crane Brinton that during "the late seventeenth century . . . there arose in our society what seems to clearly be a new religion. . . . I call this religion simply Enlightenment, with a capital E."[6] This is "the religion of the Republic," for I think it provides, or legitimates, the premises of the Declaration of Independence, the Constitution, and a long line of Supreme Court decisions on matters pertaining to religion.

Enlightenment, in Brinton's sense of the term, consists in a radical monotheism, or as one might describe Jefferson's position, a unitarianism of the First Person—Thomas Paine's "plain, pure, and unmixed belief of one God." Here "God" is an absolute presupposition, not a problem as he, or it, has apparently become even for most theologians today. Whatever else these American men of Enlightenment may have been, they were not atheists. They were "infidels" in the narrow theological sense that term then conveyed; that is, they denied that the Bible was, or contained, the sole and necessary revelation of God to man. They built upon that other strand in the Christian tradition, the concept of God's second volume of revelation—the Creation. Thomas Paine expounds this doctrine at length in his *The Age of Reason* (1794).

Where Christians argued that some men were enabled by grace to understand the revelation in Scripture, the cosmopolitan men of Enlightenment argued that all men are gifted by the Creator with "Reason" that enables them to read and understand his revelation in his creation. The two parties agreed that man's duty was to obey

God, and that he learned what his duty was by interpreting God's revelation. They disagreed on the locus and nature of the revelation.

The Reformation established in Christendom the right of private judgment, but without undermining belief in the biblical revelation as highest authority. What prevailed among Protestants was the right of private judgment *under the Scriptures*. By the end of the eighteenth century, however, the right of private judgment had, for many intellectuals, been divorced from biblical authority. For the first time in the history of Christendom a genuinely *religious* alternative to orthodox Christianity surfaced; and it has persisted and is very much alive and flourishing in the minds and hearts of Americans today. This is a commonly accepted observation. The highly visible Michael Novak noted in *The Century Magazine* for April, 1971, that "the tradition in which intellectuals ordinarily define themselves [today] is that of the Enlightenment"; indeed, he added "the dominant religion" in America *is* "the religion of the Enlightenment" and the issue between it and "an adequate contemporary religion [presumably Christianity] . . . is theological."[7] This seems to me to be what I have been trying to get theologians to see for at least twenty years.

The obverse side of the Enlightenment's high doctrine of the Creator and Governor of the universe was the finite limitation of the creature in *every* respect. This determined the conception of the nature and limits of man's knowledge. The creature could not have absolute knowledge of anything, but only "opinions" and, as James Madison argued, "the opinions of men" depend "only on the evidence contemplated in their own minds." Therefore, opinions could neither be borrowed from others nor imposed by coercion—that damnable error of religionists which, Jefferson thought, had made half the world hypocrites and the other half fools.

Madison defined religion as one's *opinion* of the "duty which we owe to our creator, and the manner of discharging it." It followed that the individual's duty was "to render the creator such homage, and such only, as he believes to be acceptable to him"— a neat way of stating the implication of the principle of the right of private judgment. Duty to the Creator, Madison continued, "is precedent, both in order of time and degree of obligation, to the claims of civil society," because "before any man can be considered as a member of civil society," he must be considered as a subject of the governor of the universe." A person's first and ultimate *"allegiance* [is] *to the universal sovereign."* A man's duty is to obey what his own conscience tells him is the will of God. In other words, one must obey God rather than men. Thus Madison categorically rejects idolatry of any human forms.

Here, then, was a radical conceptual separation of the substance or essence of religion from its tangible forms, the socially devised vehicles, of religion. John Adams's view was typical:

> The substance and essence of Christianity, as I understand it, is eternal and unchangeable, and will bear examination forever, but it has been mixed with extraneous ingredients, which I think will not bear examination, and they ought to be separated.

This could be interpreted as the embryo of the concept of "religionless Christianity." But in the Enlightenment's conception, the "substance and essence of Christianity" is the same as that of all religions.

The forms, being merely the humanly built vehicles for the conveyance of the essentials, were subject to moral judgment on the basis of their practical efficacy. So Franklin, assuming that the essentials were "to be found in all the religions we had in our country," said that he "respected them all, Tho' with different degrees of respect, as I found them . . . mix'd with other articles, which without any tendency to inspire, promote, or confirm morality, serv'd principally to divide us. . . ." We are not surprised to read that after attending the preaching of one minister on five successive Sundays, Franklin gave up when he became convinced that the minister's motive was to make good Presbyterians rather than moral citizens. It is obvious that Franklin's theology provided legitimation for the acceptance of religious pluralism in a commonwealth.

Finally, the whole structure of Enlightenment (in Brinton's sense) rested on faith in the Creator and Governor of the universe. This faith enabled Jefferson to assert in the "Act for Establishing Religious Freedom," adopted by the Virginia legislature in 1779,

> that truth is great and will prevail if left to herself, that she is the proper and sufficient antagonist to error, and has nothing to fear from the conflict, unless by human interposition disarmed of her natural weapons, free argument and debate, errors ceasing to be dangerous when it is permitted freely to contradict them.

This was hard doctrine for many orthodox Christians of the time who, in keeping with centuries of Christian thinking and practice, would use the sword of steel in defense of truth.

This, all too briefly sketched and illustrated, is what I understand by Enlightenment religion, and think to be the fountainhead of what I have called "the religion of the Republic." It seems to me to have had a definable theological structure and that it was this theology that provided legitimation for the Declaration of Independence, for the constitutional provisions concerning religion, and for the legal premises which underlie the long line of Supreme Court decisions having to do with the relation between what Madison called the rights of religion and the civil authorities in the United States.[8] What Enlightenment theology legitimated, orthodox Christian theology apparently could not at that time sustain: religious pluralism in a commonwealth.

Because the perspective of Enlightenment (still in Brinton's sense), whether in the mild form of a Joseph Priestly's unitarianism or the radical form of a Thomas Paine's deism, either denied the orthodox Christian interpretation of the Bible, or flatly denied that the Bible was or could be the only revelation from God, Christian leaders could not accept it. They remained absolutists on biblical authority. Paine rightly complained that his opponents did not recognize that he was questioning the authority itself. Such men assumed that a particularistically Christian nation was being formed along somewhat different but essentially traditional Christian lines. This assumption has been asserted in our time by proponents of the post-Protestant interpretation of American history.

Once the Constitution was accepted, national religious freedom established, and the new nation launched, Christian leaders mounted a massive attack against Enlightenment religion, which they dubbed "infidelity" but confused with atheism. This ecclesiastical counterrevolution—for that is what it amounted to—was carried on the wave of revivalism following 1795 that is known as the Second Great Awakening. In it, Enlightenment was swamped under a flood of invective that, while sweeping around the theological issue, drowned "infidelity" under a mire of social opprobrium.

At that time, Protestants turned back to pre-seventeenth-century theologies for the substance of their intellectual lives, and thus "sent the mass of men back to a set of beliefs that was bound to come into sharp conflict with the expanding world of science, and made them suspicious of any attempt at mediation or conciliation."[9] This marks the point where, as Whitehead put it, "the clergy . . . began to waver in their appeal to constructive reason" for the explanation and defense of Christian modes of thinking and acting. They surrendered the intellectual initiative to leaders of the main currents of modern thought, which were rooted in the Enlightenment; and theological education tended to become increasingly training for the maintenance of organized ecclesiastical life in an intellectual ghetto whose premises were derived from the first to the sixteenth centuries.

But what seems to me more important than the traditionally emphasized conflict between science and religion that followed in the nineteenth century is that insofar as the attack on Enlightenment monotheistic religion was successful, it undermined the theological legitimation of the constitutional and legal systems of the Republic. These, by and large, have had increasingly to look outside the churches for such support. One result of this, suggested above, has been that in defense of traditional forms of Christianity, ecclesiastical leaders in America have often appeared to be offering their members a choice between being good Christians and being good citizens.

The Christian reaction against Enlightenment is understandable historically. Against the monolithic absolutism of Christian doctrine, Enlightenment opposed what latter-day Justices of the Supreme Court have called the principle of the plurality of principles —which means that court decisions are seldom based on appeal to one legal principle.

Christian leaders sensed that acceptance of religious pluralism *in principle* foretold the passing for every religious group of its peculiar and particularistic identity. Some Protestant leaders in the early nineteenth century clearly recognized and welcomed this prospect because, they argued, the providential undermining of all sectarian particularity would permit the emergence in actuality of true Christian unity.

But the religious freedom that made all the sects voluntary associations, equal before a civil authority that was neutral where their sectarian claims were concerned, also placed them in a highly competitive relationship to one another in a vast free market of souls. This tended to induce, indeed to force each group to accentuate, its peculiar doctrinal emphases and institutional forms. For only in them could its leaders find justification for their sect's separateness from all the others. So while the principles of the commonwealth in which they lived as citizens were pushing them in the direction of recognizing their common Christianity (that is, Christianity in general), the emphasis in their churches upon heightened sectarian claims was countering this. Cosmopolitan principles were opposed to tribal principles, widening the gulf between being Christians and being citizens of the Republic.

It is important to note that the triumph of Christianity over infidelity by around 1830 was not a theological or intellectual triumph, but rather, what might well be called a great and successful campaign of character assassination. Its success was exemplified when Theodore Roosevelt called Thomas Paine a filthy little atheist. Because the theological issue was not resolved, the two parts of the culture simply went their separate ways. Since that time, the intellectual and religious lives have not only flowed in separate, albeit sometimes parallel, streams, but have been separately institutionalized in the universities and denominations respectively. Universities define the intellectual life; denominations define the religious life. This is why so many professors in university-related theological schools have split personalities.

The result of this historical development on individual church members was made vivid for me by reading a review of *A Study of Generations,* sponsored jointly by the three largest Lutheran synods. The study produced what the reviewer called a "family portrait," apparently of Oliver Cromwell's "warts and all" variety. The three researchers collected "seven million bits of information" from 4,745 Lutherans, and in a final chapter reported fifty-seven "findings." Among the latter were such discoveries as that there are differences between the generations, and between clergy and laity, and between the synods! But to me, the only significant "finding" reported by the reviewer was "that three out of four Lutherans said that all religions lead to the same God, yet three out of four . . . [also] stated that belief in Jesus Christ is absolutely necessary for salvation."[10] What is astonishing is the implication that around 50 percent of Lutheran church members in the United States find it possible simultaneously to hold two theologically contrary views, each rooted in age-old antagonistic theological traditions. To the historian the question is, How did this situation come to be?—or, more specifically, How did these Lutherans, of all people, get that way?

I have tried to adumbrate an answer. It is that these members polled are *both* Lutheran Christians and loyal citizens of the commonwealth in which they live; that the theology of their denominations is different from the theology that legitimates the constitutional and legal structure of their country; and that they cling to both theologies, accommodating them in different mental compartments. These good people are not just living "on the boundary" between two worlds of reality. They are religiously and intellectually split, part of them living in each of the two worlds at the same time. In this, of course, they reflect the split in the society itself.

Now that this split has been solemnly and scientifically demonstrated to exist even in the least theologically eroded of all the Protestant denominations, perhaps even some Lutheran theologians will turn enough of their attention from Luther and the Reformation to try to find out why this "something very curious" that the researchers noted is "going on" in their members. I think the answer lies in the peculiar experience of the old Christianity in this New World.

Epilogue

I have written these pieces with the chilling realization that we live today under the shadow of man's power to destroy all life on this planet. In a happier time of more primitive technology, James Russell Lowell could say that when God gave man a matchbox he knew that the framework of the world was fireproof. Today, with Loren Eiseley, I feel that tomorrow I may be a fleck of carbon in the rubble of that world. This would be to go out with a bang. But it is equally likely that man will end more slowly, with a whimper, in an overcrowded world and an environment so dirtied by his refusal to control the pollution of his own nest that it can no longer sustain life. There are also the terrifying possibilities lurking in chemical and biological "weapons." I agree with Arthur Goldberg that probably man now has less than a 50 percent chance of survival.

The appalling thing is that so many persons, including leaders in high places, seem to lack the imagination to perceive the possibility of the end of man. But to our youth this possibility is an ever present reality; and perhaps this is the most important element in the gap between them and so many of the older generation who seem content to conduct the business of living at the same old stands, in the same old way, and with the obsolete faith of James Russell Lowell.

Let me then close this volume with words from Shakespeare that are appropriate for all of us today:

> . . . whether we shall meet again I know not.
> Therefore our everlasting farewell take.
> For ever and for ever farewell, Cassius!
> If we do meet again, why, we shall smile;
> If not, why then this parting was well made.

Notes

PREFACE

1. Koch, *The American Enlightenment* (New York: George Braziller, 1965), p. 19.

2. Richey and Jones (eds.), *American Civil Religion* (New York: Harper & Row, 1974). With the publication of this book "The Civil Religion Debate" joins the "Honest to God," "The Secular City," and the "Death of God" debates in being embalmed in a paperback collection of articles similar to those that have marked the twilight of interest in those previous fads of the jet-set schoolmen.

3. When I first read Robert N. Bellah's now deservedly famous "Civil Religion in America" (*Daedalus,* Winter 1967, pp. 1–21), which was published at about the same time as my "The 'Nation with the Soul of a Church,' " I thought, as I still do, that here was a kindred spirit who was talking about what I preferred to call "the religion of the Republic." I agree with his way of stating the proposition: "that there actually exists alongside of and rather clearly differentiated from the churches an elaborate and well-institutionalized civil religion in America" and that "this religion . . . has its own seriousness and integrity and requires the same care in understanding that any other religion does." Bellah expressed the same kind of puzzlement that I felt: "Why [had] something so obvious . . . escaped serious analytical attention?" Immediate, widespread, continuing, and often emotional reaction to his article made it clear that what

seemed obvious to Bellah and to me was not obvious to many others. In his response to the essays in the Richey and Jones book noted above ("American Civil Religion in the 1970s," pp. 255–72) and more recently in his book, *The Broken Covenant: American Civil Religion in Time of Trial* (New York: Crossroad Book of the Seabury Press, 1975; pp. ix, 3) Bellah has spelled out what he means by "civil religion" and delineated the assumption(s) on which his conception rests. What I hear him saying makes sense to me, and I agree "for substance thereof." But my interest and purpose are different.

4. For some explanation see Mead, *The Lively Experiment: The Shaping of Christianity in America* (New York: Harper & Row, 1963). For example, pp. 55, 68.

I. IN QUEST OF AMERICA'S RELIGION

1. First published in *The Christian Century*, LXXXVII (June 17, 1970), 752–56.

2. May, in *American Historical Review*, LXX (October 1964), 79.

3. Clebsch, *From Sacred to Profane America* (New York: Harper & Row, 1968), pp. x–xi, 4.

4. Niebuhr, *The Meaning of Revelation* (New York: Macmillan, 1946), *passim*, with specific reference p. 62. Niebuhr scouted the distinction between biography and autobiography, p. 60.

5. Brown, *The Ecumenical Revolution* (New York: Doubleday, 1967), chapter 5, "The Reformation of the Interpretation of Reformation Interpretation," pp. 87–101.

6. *The Christian Century*, October 15, 1969, p. 1305.

7. Tillich, *The Theology of Culture* (New York: Oxford University Press, 1959), p. 42.

8. May, "The Recovery of American Religious History," *American Historical Review*, LXX (October 1964), 79.

9. Fielding, *The History of Tom Jones* (New York: Modern Library Edition), p. 84.

10. Tillich, *Christianity and the Encounter of the World Religions* (New York: Columbia University Press, 1963), p. 97.

11. My concept of "the Republic" is essentially that developed by Ross Lockridge, Jr., in his great novel, *Raintree County* (Boston: Houghton Mifflin Co., 1948). His most succinct statement of the concept is on p. 929:

"But Oneself exists by virtue of a world shared with other selves. Our life is the intersection of the Self with an Other. In the intense personal form this intersection is love, and in the ideal, general form it's the Republic. Jesus gives us the moral shape of this Republic—the sign of the Cross." Compare H. Richard Niebuhr: "Our past is our present in our conscious and unconscious memory. To understand such a present past is to understand one's self. . . . To remember all that is in our past and so in our present is to achieve unity of self. To remember the human past as our own past is to achieve community with mankind. . . . Without the integration of the personal and social past there can be no present integrity of the self nor anything like human brotherhood." *The Meaning of Revelation,* p. 117.

12. Camus, *The Rebel: An Essay on Man in Revolt,* trans. Anthony Bower (New York: Vintage Books, 1958), pp. 305–6.

II. THE POST-PROTESTANT CONCEPT AND AMERICA'S TWO RELIGIONS

1. First published in *Religion in Life,* XXXIII (Spring 1964), 191–204.

2. Hudson, *American Protestantism* (Chicago: University of Chicago Press, 1961).

3. Marty, *The New Shape of American Religion* (New York: Harper & Row, 1958).

4. Herberg, "Religion and Culture in Present-Day America," *Roman Catholicism and the American Way of Life,* ed. Thomas T. McAvoy (South Bend, Ind.: University of Notre Dame Press, 1960), pp. 4–9. This article is an excellent brief summary of the thesis Herberg developed extensively in his book *Protestant, Catholic, Jew* (Garden City, N.Y.: Doubleday, 1955).

5. Hudson, *American Protestantism,* p. 129.

6. *Ibid.,* p. 130.

7. *Ibid.,* p. 141.

8. *Ibid.,* p. 172 (Hudson quoting Fosdick).

9. Hudson, *The Great Tradition of the American Churches* (New York: Harper & Row, 1953), p. 252.

10. Hudson, *The Great Tradition,* p. 174.

11. Marty, *The New Shape,* p. 32.

12. *Ibid.*, p. 2.

13. *Ibid.*, p. 4.

14. *Ibid.*, p. 2.

15. *Ibid.*, p. 10.

16. *Ibid.*

17. *Ibid.*, p. 14.

18. *Ibid.*, p. 32.

19. Herberg, *Religion and Culture*, p. 7.

20. *Ibid.*, pp. 10–11.

21. *Ibid.*, p. 14.

22. *Ibid.*, pp. 11–12.

23. *Ibid.*, p. 13.

24. "Secularization" is so important in Herberg's thesis that it is necessary to note how he uses this most ambiguous word. In *Protestant, Catholic, Jew* he defines "explicit secularism" as "hostility or demonstrative indifference to religion" and notes that it "is a minor and diminishing force" in the United States (p. 287). In that definition the word "religion" is ambiguous. Apparently Herberg means by it the Jewish-Christian religion. Hence when he says secularism "is thinking and living in terms of a framework of reality and value remote from the religious beliefs simultaneously professed" (p. 14), the implication is that a framework provided by any religion other than Jewish-Christian would be a form of secularism. In brief, it would seem that to Herberg all that is not distinctively Jewish-Christian as he defines it is "secularism." Therefore, while in another connection recognizing that Americanism "has its religious creed, evoking the appropriate religious emotion" and "may, in fact, be taken as the civic religion of the American people" (p. 279), presumably because it is "secularism," one does not have to take its theology seriously.

25. Herberg, *Religion and Culture*, p. 14.

26. *Ibid.*, pp. 15–16.

27. Commager, *The American Mind* (New Haven: Yale University Press, 1950), p. 163.

28. Marty, *The New Shape*, p. 68.

29. Cf. George S. Hendry, "Knowing the Time," *Theology Today*, July 1962, pp. 157–64: "There is a curious blindness to the fact that the Christian 'assumptions' were from the first superimposed on another set of assumptions which are derived from the Enlightenment of the eighteenth century. It would have surprised the founding fathers—or the most influential among them at all events—to know that almost two centuries after their

time the question would be seriously asked whether this is the post-Christian era; for they thought they were inaugurating it. . . . But since the ideology of the Enlightenment was strictly 'post-Christian' in the same sense, though in a less disguised manner than that of Communism, the Christian frame of reference could be superimposed on it without great difficulty, and the American way of life, as it is called, is the offspring of this union, exhibiting features which derive from each of its parents."

Regarding the last sentence, see my *The Lively Experiment: The Shaping of Christianity in America* (New York: Harper & Row, 1963), p. 38.

30. By and large the theological revival beginning around 1930 sought for historical roots primarily in the right-wing tradition which never, or never as completely, digested religious freedom and pluralism as did the left-wing groups. Thomas Jefferson spoke from experience both when he commended the Baptists for their consistent advocacy of religious freedom and when he said of the right-wing New England clergy that "the advocate of religious freedom is to expect neither peace nor forgiveness from them." In this connection see my review of R. Freeman Butts, *The American Tradition in Religion and Education,* in *The Journal of Religion,* April 1952, p. 143.

31. Chesterton lists the following: "Are you an anarchist? . . . Are you in favour of subverting the government of the United States by force? . . . Are you a polygamist?" All the quotations from Chesterton are taken from Raymond T. Bond (ed.), *The Man Who Was Chesterton* (Garden City, N.Y.: Doubleday Image Books, 1960).

32. Bond, *The Man Who Was Chesterton,* pp. 125–26.

33. The literature on this point is very extensive. Reference to much of it will be found in chapter 3 of Mead, *The Lively Experiment.*

34. Marty, *The New Shape,* p. 84. In an article in the December 1962 issue of *This Day* Marty noted one who "upheld the viewpoint that America never was Protestant; it was rationalist (as were Franklin, Jefferson, Washington, and many other founding Fathers)," and acknowledged that "America may have been officially born under those auspices. But the nineteenth century, I believe, produced a new setting. The United States became Protestant." The statement illustrates the confusion of referents that is built into the discussion of "post-Protestant" America. When it is said that "America never was Protestant; it was rationalist," the referent must be the substratum of assumptions underlying the Declaration, etc., for non-Protestant groups were negligible. But when Marty says the United States "became Protestant" in the nineteenth century, I think the

referent must be the prevailing influence of Protestantism, not the substratum of assumptions. Surely Marty does not mean that the Declaration was converted and baptized by Protestants so that its assumptions were Christianized!

35. By "classical sense" I mean the sense in which "secularism" was used by G. J. Holyoake and others around the middle of the nineteenth century—"the doctrine that morality should be based solely in regard to the well-being of mankind in the present life, to the exclusion of all considerations drawn from belief in God or in future life." See Leroy E. Loemker, "The Nature of Secularism," in J. Richard Spann (ed.), *The Christian Faith and Secularism* (Nashville: Abingdon-Cokesbury Press, 1948), p. 12.

36. In Frank Luther Mott and Chester E. Jorgenson (eds.), *Benjamin Franklin; Representative Selections. . . .* (New York: American Book Co., 1936), pp. 69–70.

37. It is to be noted that at the time when the United States, from the post-Protestant perspective, was, or was becoming, wholly "Protestant," European visitors were commonly struck by the observance of the national religion. For example, Francis J. Grund in his *The Americans in Their Moral, Social and Political Relations* (1837): "It is with the solemnities of religion that the Declaration of Independence is yet annually read to the people from the pulpit, or that Americans celebrate the anniversaries of the most important events in their history. It is to religion they have recourse whenever they wish to impress the popular feeling with anything relative to their country; and it is religion which assists them in all their national undertakings."

38. Sugrue, *A Catholic Speaks His Mind on America's Religious Conflict* (New York: Harper & Row, 1951). Sugrue's point here bears out Herberg's observation that "the authentic content of faith may even prove a serious handicap" to assimilation as "American."

39. *Ibid.,* p. 43.

40. *Ibid.,* p. 20.

41. Strong, *Our Country: Its Possible Future and Its Present Crisis* (New York: Baker & Taylor Co., 1891), pp. 101–2.

42. Herberg, *Protestant, Catholic, Jew,* p. 274.

43. Marty, *The New Shape,* p. 72.

44. *Ibid.,* pp. 71–72.

45. Marty, *The Infidel* (New York: Meridian Books, 1961), pp. 21, 16.

46. Winthrop S. Hudson, "Denominationalism as a Basis for Ecumeni-

city: A Seventeenth-Century Conception," *Church History,* XXIV (March 1955), 32–50. See also *American Protestantism* (Chicago: University of Chicago Press, 1961), pp. 33–48.

47. This stumbling block has been recognized by contemporary ecumenical leaders, e.g., "The final and terrible difficulty is that Churches cannot unite, unless they are willing to die. In a truly united Church, there would be no more Anglicans or Lutherans or Presbyterians or Methodists." Ruth Rouse and Stephen Charles Neill (eds.), *A History of the Ecumenical Movement 1517–1948* (2d ed.; Philadelphia: The Westminster Press, 1967), p. 495. This theme is picked up by Brown, *The Ecumenical Revolution,* pp. 135ff.

48. Ronald E. Osborn, *The Spirit of American Christianity* (New York: Harper & Row, 1958), pp. 137–38.

III. THE FACT OF PLURALISM AND THE PERSISTENCE OF SECTARIANISM

1. First published in Elwyn A. Smith (ed.), *The Religion of the Republic* (Philadelphia: Fortress Press, 1971), pp. 247–66.

2. Philip Schaff, *America: A Sketch of Its Political, Social, and Religious Character,* ed. Perry Miller (Cambridge, Mass.: Belknap Press of Harvard University Press, 1961), p. 80.

3. Justice Brennan, concurring opinion in the Murray-Schempp decision of June 17, 1963, *The Bible and the Public Schools . . . the Full Text of the Majority Concurring and Dissenting Opinions of the Court . . .* (New York: Liberal Press, 1963), pp. 95–96.

4. Reinhold Niebuhr, "A Note on Pluralism," *Religion in America: Original Essays on Religion in a Free Society,* ed. John Cogley (New York: Meridian Books, 1958), p. 43. See also Crane Brinton, *The Shaping of the Modern Mind* (New York: New American Library, 1953 [paperback]), p. 66. *The Shaping of the Modern Mind* is the concluding half of *Men and Ideas* (originally pub. Englewood Cliffs, N.J.: Prentice-Hall, 1950 and 1953).

5. The common legal view seems to be that the "provisions of the code for the incorporation of churches or religious societies, and all powers conferred thereunder, relate alone to their properties or temporalities, and have no reference to the churches or societies as such, which bodies, as spiritual or ecclesiastical organizations, exist independent of their charters."

Therefore "wherever there is an incorporated church, there are two entities, the one, the church as such, not owing its ecclesiastical or spiritual existence to the civil law, and the legal corporation, each separate though closely allied." Quoted in John J. McGrath, *Church and State in American Law: Cases and Materials* (Milwaukee: Bruce Publishing Co., 1962), pp. 5–6. See also my "Neither Church nor State: Reflections on James Madison's 'Line of Separation,' " this volume, pp. 78–94.

6. Alfred North Whitehead, *Adventures of Ideas* (New York: a Mentor Book, 1955), pp. 158–59.

7. This seems to me one way of looking at the difference between the "progressive" and "conservative" church-state views of contemporary Roman Catholics, which are so clearly presented by Thomas T. Love, *John Courtney Murray: Contemporary Church-State Theory* (Garden City, N.Y.: Doubleday, 1965). Central in Murray's position was his insistence that modern "lay" democracy (limited) was something new and to be distinguished from nineteenth-century "laic" democracy (absolutistic). This was what induced him to make his tremendous reexamination of his church's inherited conceptual order.

8. See, e.g., Mr. Justice Clark's opinion of the court in the Murray-Schempp decision; in Arthur Frommer (ed.), *The Bible and the Public Schools* (New York: Liberal Press, 1963), pp. 77–78.

9. Federal Communications Commission, quoted in Anson Phelps Stokes, *Church and State in the United States* (New York: Harper & Row, 1950), vol. 3, p. 246.

10. James Baldwin, "The Discovery of What It Means to Be an American," *Nobody Knows My Name* (New York: Dell Publishing Co., 1963). This essay was first published in the *New York Times Book Review*, January 25, 1959.

11. Whitehead, *Adventures of Ideas*, pp. 19–20.

12. Ruth Benedict, *Patterns of Culture* (originally pub. 1934), with a new preface by Margaret Mead (Boston: Houghton Mifflin Co., 1959), p. 16.

13. Adolf A. Berle, Jr., *Power without Property: A New Development in American Political Economy* (New York: Harcourt, Brace, & World, 1959), pp. 110–16.

14. Ralph Henry Gabriel, *The Course of American Democratic Thought* (2d ed.; New York: Ronald Press, 1956), chapters 2 and 3, pp. 12–39. Specific reference, p. 26.

15. Whitehead, *Adventures of Ideas*, pp. 19–20. Mr. Justice Frankfurter

said (*Minersville School District* v. *Gobitis*, 310 U.S. 568 [1940]), " 'We live by symbols.' The flag is the symbol of our national unity, transcending all internal differences, however large, within the framework of the Constitution. This Court has had occasion to say that '. . . the flag is the symbol of the Nation's power, the emblem of freedom in its truest, best sense. . . . it signifies government resting on the consent of the governed; liberty regulated by law; the protection of the weak against the strong; security against the exercise of arbitrary power; and absolute safety for free institutions against foreign aggression.' *Halter* v. *Nebraska*." In Joseph Tussman (ed.), *The Supreme Court on Church and State* (New York: Oxford University Press, 1962), p. 83.

16. Whitehead, *Adventures of Ideas,* p. 175.

17. Lyman Beecher, "Resources of the Adversary and Means of Their Destruction" (1827), in *Sermons Delivered on Various Occasions* (Boston: T. R. Marvin, 1828), p. 268.

18. Wilhelm Pauck, "Our Protestant Heritage," in *Religion and Contemporary Society,* ed. Harold Stahmer (New York: Macmillan, 1963), p. 92.

19. Leonard Woolsey Bacon, *A History of American Christianity* (New York: Charles Scribner's Sons, 1895), p. 404.

20. See, e.g., Wilhelm Pauck, "Theology in the Life of Contemporary American Protestantism," *Shane Quarterly,* 13 (1952), 37–50; Joseph Haroutunian, "Theology and American Experience," *Criterion,* 3 (1964), 1–10; and John Tracy Ellis, *American Catholics and the Intellectual Life* (Chicago: Heritage Foundation, 1956).

21. Pauck, "Our Protestant Heritage," pp. 108–9.

22. Will Herberg, "Religion and Culture in Present-Day America," in *Roman Catholicism and the American Way of Life,* ed. Thomas T. McAvoy (Notre Dame, Ind.: University of Notre Dame Press, 1960), p. 15.

23. Loren P. Beth, *The American Theory of Church and State* (Gainesville: University of Florida Press, 1958), pp. 141–42.

24. Albert G. Huegli (ed.), *Church and State Under God* (St. Louis: Concordia Publishing House, 1964), p. 436.

25. Gunnar Myrdal, *An American Dilemma: The Negro Problem and Modern Democracy* (New York: Harper & Row, 1944), p. xlvii. In the book this passage is italicized.

26. Charles Hodge, "The Unity of the Church Based on Personal Union with Christ," *Documents of the Sixth General Conference of the Evangelical Alliance, Held in New York, October 2–12, 1873,* ed. Philip Schaff

and S. Irenaeus Prime (New York: Harper & Row, 1874), pp. 139–44. Hereafter cited as *E. A. Conference, 1873.*

27. "Theories of the Church," *The Biblical Repertory and Princeton Review 18* (1846), 148. This article is a clear statement of the evangelical's doctrine of the church as distinguished from the "ritualistic" and the "rationalistic" views.

28. Eliphalet Nott Potter, "The Communion of Saints: Modes of Its Promotion and Manifestation," *E. A. Conference, 1873,* p. 156.

29. Philip Schaff, "Religion in the United States of America," in *The Religious Condition of Christendom Described in a Series of Papers Presented to the Seventh General Conference of the Evangelical Alliance, Held in Basle, 1879,* ed. J. Murray Mitchell (London: Hodder & Stoughton, 1880), p. 90.

30. Of course, as Winthrop S. Hudson has made clear, the evangelical stance in the nineteenth century was rooted in the revivalistic movement of the eighteenth, and before that, in the thinking of some of the Independent Divines of the seventeenth century. (*American Protestantism* [Chicago: University of Chicago Press, 1961], chap. 1, sec. 3. Note especially Hudson's quotations from Gilbert Tennent, Samuel Davies, and George Whitefield.)

I have wondered why the evangelical movement with its fine and useful distinctions became an almost forgotten chapter of American church history, and why sectarianism came so largely to prevail.

31. This was implied in both the rationalistic and the pietistic movements of the eighteenth century. This was what enabled them on the issue of religious freedom to combine against the particularist traditionalists. See my *The Lively Experiment: The Shaping of Christianity in America* (New York: Harper & Row, 1963), pp. 38–41.

32. *Evangelical Alliance: Report of the Proceedings of the Conference, Held at Freemasons' Hall, London, from August Nineteenth to September Second, Inclusive, 1846* (London: Partridge & Oakey, 1847), p. 87.

33. Schaff, *America: A Sketch of Its Political, Social, and Religious Character,* pp. 80–81. *America . . .* was first published in 1855.

34. Ruth Rouse and Stephen Charles Neill (ed.), *A History of the Ecumenical Movement 1517–1948,* 2d ed., with rev. bib. (Philadelphia: Westminster Press, 1967), p. 495.

35. See chapter II, above, "The Post-Protestant Concept and America's Two Religions," pp. 11–28.

For some American churchmen ecumenism and merger have taken their place beside "mother, home and heaven" as things not to be criticized. It may be salutary for those insiders who believe, rightly, that "ecumenicity is a great and exciting reality in our time" to see themselves as some profane outsiders saw them in 1965 and drew their portrait in the popular journalistic venture from which I have drawn much of what follows.

36. Lee E. Dirks (ed.), *Religion in Action: How America's Faiths Are Meeting New Challenges* (Silver Spring, Md.: National Observer, 1965), p. 19. The following eight quotations are taken from this work, pp. 14, 16, 19, 25, 22, and 24, in that order.

IV. THE "NATION WITH THE SOUL OF A CHURCH"

1. First published in *Church History*, XXXVI (September 1967), 1–22.
2. Raymond T. Bond (ed.), *The Man Who Was Chesterton* (Garden City, N.Y.: Doubleday Image Books, 1960), p. 131.
3. *Ibid.*, p. 132.
4. Ernest Barker, "Christianity and Nationalism" [1927], *Church, State, and Education* (Ann Arbor: University of Michigan Press, 1957), p. 131.
5. Barker, *op. cit.*, p. 132. The quotations in the following two paragraphs are taken from this book, pp. 133–36.
6. *Ibid.*, p. 136.
7. I quote from the edition published by the Congregational Board of Publications, Boston, 1860, pp. 39–40.
8. Barker, *op. cit.*, p. 138. William Temple, *Citizen and Churchman* (London: Eyre & Spottiswoode, 1941), p. 68.
9. Barker, *op. cit.*, pp. 138–39.
10. Crane Brinton, *The Shaping of the Modern Mind* (New York: Mentor Books, 1953), pp. 59–61.
11. Ellis, *American Catholicism* (Chicago: University of Chicago Press, 1955), p. 50.
12. Barker, *op. cit.*, p. 140.
13. Cox, *The Secular City* (New York: Macmillan, 1965), p. 105.
14. Schaff, *America: A Sketch of Its Political, Social, and Religious Character*, ed. Perry Miller (Cambridge: Belknap Press of the Harvard University Press, 1961), p. 88. First published 1855.
15. Alexander Dru (ed. and trans.), *The Journals of Søren Kierkegaard* (London: Oxford University Press, 1938), p. 184.

16. See Perry Miller and Thomas H. Johnson, *The Puritans* (New York: American Book Co., 1938), p. 187; Perry Miller, *Errand into the Wilderness* (Cambridge: Belknap Press of the Harvard University Press, 1956), pp. 146–47.

17. See the Cambridge Platform of 1648, chap. X, sect. 3, in Williston Walker, *The Creeds and Platforms of Congregationalism* (Boston: Pilgrim Press, 1960), p. 217. First published 1893.

18. Wise, *Vindication of the Government of the New England Churches*, p. 29 (1717). A facsimile reproduction with an introduction by Perry Miller (Gainesville, Fla.: Scholars' Facsimiles and Reprints, 1958).

19. Robert H. Jackson, *The Supreme Court in the American System of Government* (New York: Harper & Row, 1963), pp. 2–3.

20. Baird, *Religion in America* (New York: Harper & Row, 1845), p. 119.

21. Mr. Justice Black's dissenting opinion in *Zorach* v. *Clauson,* in Joseph Tussman (ed.), *The Supreme Court on Church & State* (New York: Oxford University Press, 1962), pp. 270–71.

22. Granted that "the fact is that the line which separates the secular from the sectarian in the American way of life is elusive," as Mr. Justice Brennan noted in his concurring opinion in the Schempp-Murray case; in Arthur Frommer (ed.), *The Bible and the Public Schools* (New York: Liberal Press, 1963), p. 86.

23. Niebuhr, "The Commitment of the Self and the Freedom of the Mind," in *Religion & Freedom of Thought,* ed. Perry Miller *et al.* (Garden City, N.Y.: Doubleday, 1954), p. 59.

24. John R. G. Hassard, *Life of the Most Reverend John Hughes D.D., First Archbishop of New York. With Extracts from His Private Correspondence* (New York: D. Appleton and Co., 1866), p. 226.

25. Quoted in H. Shelton Smith, Robert T. Handy, and Lefferts A. Loetscher, *American Christianity,* I (New York: Charles Scribner's Sons, 1960), 394.

26. Whitehead, *Adventures of Ideas* (New York: Mentor Books, 1955), p. 25.
Compare Lancelot Law Whyte, *The Next Development in Man* (New York: Mentor Books, 1949), pp. 220–21: "The universality of the formative process, once recognized and accepted, casts its spell over man. Every element finds its place in the system of nature, and every particular form symbolizes a general form. Man is himself the supreme symbol, the richest

of natural systems. Words are symbols spoken by man, but in the unitary world every form is a symbol and speaks to man."

27. Thomas Jefferson, "Notes on Virginia," in *Cornerstones of Religious Freedom in America*, ed. Joseph L. Blau (rev. ed.; New York: Harper Torchbooks, 1964), p. 82.

28. *Ibid.*, p. 83.

29. See above, pp. 21–22, for Franklin's delineation of these specific notions, and p. 24 for Josiah Strong's brief statement of them.

30. Tillich, *Christianity and the Encounter of the World Religions* (New York: Columbia University Press, 1963), pp. 96–97.

31. Bond, *The Man Who Was Chesterton* (Garden City, N.Y.: Doubleday Image Books, 1960), p. 129.

32. Schaff, *America*, 45–46.

33. "The ultimate foundation of a free society is the binding tie of cohesive sentiment. Such a sentiment is fostered by all those agencies of the mind and spirit which may serve to gather up the traditions of a people, transmit them from generation to generation, and thereby create that continuity of a treasured common life which constitutes a civilization. 'We live by symbols.' The flag is the symbol of our national unity, transcending all internal differences, however large, within the framework of the Constitution. This Court has had occasion to say that '. . . the flag is the symbol' of the Nation's power, the emblem of freedom in its truest, best sense. . . . it signifies government resting on the consent of the governed; liberty regulated by law; the protection of the weak against the strong; security against the exercise of arbitrary power; and absolute safety for free institutions against foreign aggression.' " Mr. Justice Frankfurter, opinion of the Supreme Court in the Gobitis case, 1940. In Tussman, *The Supreme Court*, p. 83.

34. Barker, "Christianity and Nationalism," p. 147.

35. *Ibid.*, p. 142.

36. Tillich, *Theology of Culture*, ed. Robert C. Kimball (New York: Oxford University Press Galaxy Books, 1964), p. 47.

37. Herberg, *Protestant, Catholic, Jew: An Essay in American Religious Sociology* (New York: Doubleday Anchor Books, 1960), pp. 74–81.

38. Whitehead, *Adventures of Ideas*, p. 26.

39. *The Christian Century*, March 2, 1966, p. 85.

40. *Criterion*, III (Winter 1964), 7.

41. Whitehead, *Adventures of Ideas*, p. 25.

42. Frommer, *The Bible and the Public Schools,* p. 65.

43. Tussman, *The Supreme Court,* p. 203.

44. *Theology Today,* XX (October 1963), 313.

45. Lucy Mack Smith, mother of the prophet Joseph Smith, stated this effect very clearly. "If," she argued, "I remain a member of no church all religious people will say I am of the world; and, if I join some one of the different denominations, all the rest will say I am in error. No church will admit that I am right, except the one with which I am associated. This makes them witnesses against each other; and how can I decide in such a case as this, seeing they are all unlike the church of Christ, as it existed in former days!" *Biographical Sketches of Joseph Smith the Prophet and His Progenitors for Many Generations* (Lamoni, Iowa: Reorganized Church of Jesus Christ of Latter-Day Saints, 1912), p. 12.

In this context it is not surprising that when the "personages" first appeared to Joseph Smith, he says, "I asked the personages who stood above me in the light which of all the sects was right—and which I should join. I was answered that I must join none of them, for they were all wrong."

46. As did also Thomas Paine, who said in the second paragraph of *The Age of Reason* (1794) that "The circumstance that has now taken place in France, of the total abolition of the whole national order of priesthood and of everything pertaining to compulsive systems of religion, and compulsive articles of faith, has not only precipitated my intention, but rendered a work of this kind exceedingly necessary; lest, in the general wreck of superstition, of false systems of government, and false theology, we lose sight of morality, of humanity, and of the theology that is true."

47. Paine complained in Part 2 of *The Age of Reason* that "all my opponents resort more or less to what they call Scripture evidence and Bible authority to help them out. They are so little masters of the subject as to confound a dispute about authenticity with a dispute about doctrines; . . ."

48. Quoted in Sidney E. Mead, *Nathaniel William Taylor 1786–1858* (Chicago: University of Chicago Press, 1942), pp. 44, 45–46.

49. Marty, *The Infidel: Free Thought and American Religion* (New York: Meridian Books, 1961), pp. 16, 203.

50. *Theology Today,* XX (October 1963), 313–21.

51. "The Memory of Our Fathers," in Beecher, *Sermons Delivered on Various Occasions* (Boston: T. R. Marvin, 1828), pp. 301–2, 304, 305.

52. Nor did many of Beecher's contemporaries. "The American civil religion was never anticlerical or militantly secular. On the contrary, it borrowed selectively from the religious tradition in such a way that the average American saw no conflict between the two." Robert N. Bellah, "Civil Religion in America," *Daedalus,* Winter 1967, p. 13.

53. *Theology Today,* XX (October 1963), 314.

54. Beecher, *A Plea for the West* (Cincinnati: Truman & Smith, 1835), p. 10. Beecher's sentiment was shared by most of the evangelicals. To take one example, his contemporary, S. S. Schmucker, president of the Lutheran seminary at Gettysburg, argued that "this country . . . is the chosen theatre of God for the free, unbiased development of humanity, and the settlement of the highest questions regarding its privileges, capacities and duties, in social, political and religious life." *The American Lutheran Church, Historically, Doctrinally, and Practically Delineated* (Springfield: D. Harbaugh, 1852), p. 235.

55. Roy P. Basler (ed.), *The Collected Works of Abraham Lincoln,* IV (New Brunswick: Rutgers University Press, 1953), 193–94.

56. Cushing, "Can Christians Really Unite?" *Dominion,* January 1966, pp. 19, 21.

57. *Ibid.,* p. 19.

58. Paul Tillich, *The Protestant Era,* trans. James Luther Adams (Chicago: University of Chicago Press, 1948), p. 56.

59. Strong, *Our Country,* pp. 208–10, 214, 22.

60. Camus, *The Rebel: An Essay on Man in Revolt,* trans. Anthony Bower (New York: Vintage Books, 1958), p. 299.

61. *Ibid.,* pp. 305–6.

V. NEITHER CHURCH NOR STATE: REFLECTIONS ON JAMES MADISON'S "LINE OF SEPARATION"

1. Originally published in *Journal of Church and State,* X (Autumn 1968), 349–63.

2. Paul G. Kauper, *Religion and the Constitution* (Baton Rouge: Louisiana State University Press, 1964), p. 3.

3. From a letter by Madison to the Rev. Jasper Adams, in John F. Wilson (ed.), *Church & State in American History* (Boston: D. C. Heath, 1965), pp. 77, 78.

4. William O. Douglas, "In Defense of Dissent," *The Supreme Court: Views from Inside,* ed. Alan F. Westin (New York: W. W. Norton, 1965), p. 52.

5. Robert H. Jackson, *The Supreme Court in the American System of Government* (New York: Harper Torchbooks, 1963), p. 23.

6. Harry W. Jones, "Church-State Relations: Our Constitutional Heritage," *Religion & Contemporary Society,* ed. Harold Stahmer (New York: Macmillan, 1963), p. 168.

7. Felix Frankfurter, "The Process of Judging in the Supreme Court," in Westin, *The Supreme Court,* p. 43.

8. Jones, "Church-State Relations," pp. 168–69.

9. Jackson, *The Supreme Court,* pp. 17–19.

10. Frankfurter, "The Process of Judging," p. 44.

11. Quoted by Frankfurter, *ibid.,* pp. 43–44. Italics added.

12. Quoted in Douglas, "In Defense of Dissent," p. 55.

13. Arthur Frommer (ed.), *The Bible and the Public Schools* (New York: Liberal Press, 1963), pp. 68–69. Full text of *Abington School District* v. *Schempp* and *Murray* v. *Curlett,* 374, U.S. 203 (1963) to be found in *ibid.,* pp. 57–79 and *A Journal of Church and State,* V (November 1963), 280–90.

14. *Hundley* v. *Collins,* 131 Ala. 234, 32 S. 575 (1902), in John J. McGrath (ed.), *Church and State in American Law: Cases and Materials* (Milwaukee: Bruce Publishing Co., 1962), p. 9.

15. *Kedroff* v. *St. Nicholas Cathedral,* 344 U.S. 94 (1952), in Joseph Tussman (ed.), *The Supreme Court on Church and State* (New York: Oxford University Press, 1962), pp. 298ff.

16. McGrath, *Church and State,* p. 6.

17. *West Virginia State Board of Education* v. *Barnette,* 319 U.S. 624 (1943), in Tussman, *The Supreme Court,* p. 149.

18. Clyde A. Holbrook, "Religious Scholarship and the Court," *The Christian Century,* LXXX (September 4, 1963), 1076–78. And see my reply in *ibid.,* LXXX (October 30, 1963), 1342–43.

19. For the ideas and quotations from Blackstone in the paragraph I am indebted to Robert Green McCloskey (ed.), *The Works of James Wilson,* I (Cambridge, Mass.: The Belknap Press of Harvard University Press, 1967), 168–69.

20. John Locke, *Second Treatise of Government,* chap. xi, sect. 134, *Locke's Two Treatises of Government,* ed. Peter Laslett (New York: Mentor Books, 1965), p. 401.

21. *Ibid.,* chap. xiii, sect. 149, p. 413.

22. *Ibid.,* chap. xix, sect. 213, p. 456.

23. *Ibid.,* chap. xix, sect. 222, pp. 460–61.

24. *Ibid.,* chap. xii, sect. 155, p. 417.

25. Alexis de Tocqueville, *Democracy in America,* ed. J. P. Mayer and Max Lerner, trans. George Laurence, I (New York: Harper & Row, 1966), chap. 4.

26. The ideas and quotations in this paragraph are taken from Adrienne Koch, *Madison's "Advice to My Country"* (Princeton: Princeton University Press, 1966), pp. 93–95.

27. Lyman Beecher (1775–1863) was clear that what Tocqueville called "the dogma of the sovereignty of the people" meant that there was no longer a "state" in the traditional sense, and therefore that "public opinion" was the real ruler or "executive" in the Republic. Therefore, he argued, the churches must rethink their relationship to this new situation, and much of his thought, speaking, and publication was devoted to this task. He suggests a theologically oriented view of the role of the churches in this new kind of Republic which, I think, still suggests viable guidelines.

28. Locke, *Second Treatise,* chap. xiii, sect. 149, in Laslett, *op. cit.,* pp. 412–13. Locke was very clear on this point: "Though, as I said, the *Executive* and *Federative* Power of every Community be really distinct in themselves, yet they are hardly to be separated, and placed, at the same time, in the hands of distinct Persons. For both of them requiring the force of the Society for their exercise, it is almost impracticable to place the Force of the Commonwealth in distinct, and not subordinate hands; or that the *Executive* and *Federative Power* should be placed in Persons that might act separately, whereby the Force of the Publick would be under different Commands; which would be apt sometime or other to cause disorder and ruine" (chap. xii, sect. 148, p. 412).

29. Frankfurter, "The Process of Judging," p. 35.

30. *Ibid.*

31. William J. Brennan, Jr., "State Court Decisions and the Supreme Court," in Westin, *The Supreme Court,* p. 103.

32. Jackson, *The Supreme Court,* p. 9.

33. *Ibid.,* p. 12.

34. Frommer, *The Bible and the Public Schools,* p. 27.

VI. RELIGION, CONSTITUTIONAL FEDERALISM, RIGHTS, AND THE COURT

1. Originally published in *Journal of Church and State*, XIV (Summer 1972), 191–209, and used here by permission.

2. Robert H. Jackson, *The Supreme Court in the American System of Government* (New York: Harper & Row, 1963), p. 27.

3. Philip Schaff, *America: A Sketch of Its Political, Social and Religious Character*, ed. Perry Miller (Cambridge, Mass.: Belknap Press of Harvard University Press, 1961), p. 20.

4. The use of traditional church-state terminology is a chief source of confusion when applied to the situation in the United States. For a summary view see chapter V, above, "Neither Church nor State: Reflections on James Madison's 'Line of Separation,' " pp. 78–94.

5. Jones, "Church-State Relations: Our Constitutional Heritage," in *Religion and Contemporary Society*, ed. Harold Stahmer (New York: Macmillan, 1963), p. 158.

6. For what I mean by "sectarianism" see chapter III, above, "The Fact of Pluralism and the Persistence of Sectarianism," pp. 29–47.

7. Adolph A. Berle, Jr., *Power without Property: A New Development in American Political Economy* (New York: Harcourt, Brace, & World Harvest Books, 1959), pp. 90, 91, 110–16.

8. Virginia Presbyterian Petition of 1776 as quoted in H. Shelton Smith, Robert T. Handy, and Lefferts A. Loetscher, *American Christianity: An Historical Interpretation with Representative Documents*, 2 vols. (New York: Charles Scribner's Sons, 1960), 1:445.

9. "But I say unto you, Love your enemies, bless them that curse you, do good to them that hate you, and pray for them which despitefully use you, and persecute you."

10. Cf. Wilhelm Pauck, *The Heritage of the Reformation* (Glencoe, Ill.: Free Press, 1950), p. 230: ". . . the separation of the church from the state was primarily due to the initiative of the modern state and not of the church." See also my *The Lively Experiment: The Shaping of Christianity in America* (New York: Harper & Row, 1963), pp. 20–22, 26, 27.

11. Martin Luther King, Jr., in a speech at Grinnell College, reported in the *Iowa City Press-Citizen*, October 30, 1967.

12. Robert H. Jackson, "The Supreme Court as a Political Institution," in *The Supreme Court: Views from Inside*, ed. Alan F. Westin (New York: W.W. Norton, 1961), p. 163.

13. James Madison's Fifty-First Federalist Paper contains the classic statement of the difference between "a single republic" and the "compound republic" (federalism) of the United States. Clinton Rossiter (ed.), *The Federalist Papers* (New York: New American Library Mentor Books, 1961), p. 323.

14. Felix Frankfurter, "The Process of Judging in the Supreme Court," Westin, *The Supreme Court*, p. 35.

15. *Ibid.*, p. 109.

16. Perry Miller and Thomas H. Johnson (eds.), *The Puritans* (New York: American Book Co., 1938), p. 187.

17. As quoted in Karl Herbert Hertz, "Bible Commonwealth and Holy Experiment: A Study of the Relations between Theology and Politics in the Puritan and Quaker Colonies" (Ph.D. dissertation, University of Chicago, n.d.), p. 107.

18. As quoted in *ibid.*, p. 188.

19. Compare William Temple: "It is now generally recognised that theories of a Social Contract cannot in any case be more than mythological; probably this was the intention of their several authors. There never was a moment when a contract was made. But a contract between Sovereign and people is implicit in their relations to one another." *Citizen and Churchman* (London: Eyre & Spottiswoode, 1941), p. 24. For some, America apparently made the image of a state of nature real. John Locke in discussing property in money declared, "Thus in the beginning all the World was *America, . . .* for no such thing as *Money* was anywhere known." "An Essay Concerning the True Original Extent, and End of Civil Government" (*The Second Treatise of Government,* chap. 5, sect. 49, in Peter Laslett [ed.], *John Locke, Two Treatises of Government: A Critical Edition with An Introduction and Apparatus Criticus* [New York: New American Library, 1965]), p. 343.

20. Locke, *ibid.,* p. 328.

21. *Ibid.,* p. 405.

22. *Ibid.,* p. 476.

23. This might receive literal application as with the Rev. John Davenport who argued that in an election "There are not two several and distinct actions, one of God, another of the People; but in one and the same action God, by the Peoples suffrages, makes such an one Governour, or Magistrate, and not another." As quoted in Miller and Johnson, *The Puritans,* p. 109. It was not supposed that such magistrates had divinely given wisdom for ruling. John Winthrop reminded the people ". . . to consider,

that when you choose magistrates, you take them from among yourselves, men subject to like passions as you are. . . . When you call one to be a magistrate he doth not profess nor undertake to have sufficient skill for that office, nor can you furnish him with gifts, etc., therefore you must run the hazard of his skill and ability." From Winthrop's speech to the General Court, 3 July 1645, in Miller and Johnson, *op. cit.,* p. 206.

24. The emphasis on the revolutionary right tended to fall into disrepute, and citizens have been penalized for mentioning it. "Rodger Baldwin, director of the American Civil Liberties Union, was arrested when he started to read the Declaration of Independence in front of the city hall in Paterson [New Jersey] and was convicted of conducting an unlawful assembly." Leo Pfeffer, *The Liberties of an American: The Supreme Court Speaks* (2d ed.; Boston: Beacon Press, 1963), p. 106.

25. In the Zorach case (1952) Justice Douglas argued that "Government may not . . . blend secular and sectarian education." Here "secular" means simply "nonsectarian." This meaning seems apt in the context of pluralism. Here is rooted the concept of "neutrality" which the Justices invoked in the Schempp-Murray decision of June 17, 1963: "The government is neutral, and, while protecting all, it prefers none, and it disparages none," and "in the relationship between man and religion, the State is firmly committed to a position of neutrality." Arthur Frommer (ed.), *The Bible and the Public Schools* (New York: Liberal Press, 1963), pp. 67, 69.

26. As quoted in Joseph L. Blau (ed.), *Cornerstones of Religious Freedom in America* (New York: Harper & Row, 1949), p. 107.

27. Compare Elwyn A. Smith, "Religious Liberty as a Secular Concept," *Journal of Ecumenical Studies,* 2 (Spring 1965), 275.

28. Ernest Barker, *Church, State and Education* (Ann Arbor: University of Michigan Press, 1957), p. 139.

29. Noted by Locke in Laslett, *John Locke,* p. 469.

30. *Ibid.,* p. 472.

31. *Ibid.,* p. 403. For a scholarly discussion of what I have called the inversion of the view of the flow of God's power that ushers in modern democracy, see Walter Ullman, *Principles of Government and Politics in the Middle Ages* (New York: Barnes & Noble, 1966), pp. 19–26.

32. Laslett, *John Locke,* p. 461.

33. *Ibid.,* p. 328.

34. Thomas Jefferson, "Notes on Religion," *The Complete Jefferson: Containing His Major Writings, Published and Unpublished Except His*

Letters, ed. Saul K. Padover (New York: Duell, Sloan & Pearce, 1943), pp. 943, 944.

35. Jackson, "The Supreme Court," pp. 4, 77.

36. *West Virginia State Board of Education* v. *Barnette,* 319 U.S. 624 (1943), *The Supreme Court on Church and State,* ed. Joseph Tussman (New York: Oxford University Press, 1962), p. 148. This passage was quoted by Justice Clark in his Murray-Schempp opinion. Frommer, *The Bible and the Public Schools,* p. 79.

37. Jackson in opinion in *Douglas v. City of Jeannette,* 319 U.S. 157 (1943), as found in Tussman, *The Supreme Court,* p. 140.

38. Harry Jones, "Church-State Relations: Our Constitutional Heritage," Stahmer, *Religion and Contemporary Society,* p. 166.

39. Tussman, *The Supreme Court,* pp. 147, 148.

40. Majority opinion, Murray-Schempp case, in Frommer, *The Bible and the Public Schools,* p. 78.

41. Philip Van Doren Stern (ed.), *The Life and Writings of Abraham Lincoln* (New York: Modern Library, 1940), p. 652.

42. Jones, "Church-State Relations," p. 158.

43. Jackson, "The Supreme Court," p. 9.

44. *Ibid.,* p. 10.

45. *Ibid.,* pp. 10–13. McCloskey, *The American Supreme Court,* pp. 3, 4.

46. Jackson, "The Supreme Court," p. 22.

47. *Ibid.,* p. 57.

48. *Ibid.,* p. 12.

49. Westin, *The Supreme Court,* pp. 34, 54.

50. Jackson, "The Supreme Court," pp. 13, 14. Westin, *op. cit.,* pp. 104, 108.

51. Jackson, "The Supreme Court," p. 23.

52. Westin, *The Supreme Court,* p. 54.

53. Jackson, "The Supreme Court," p. 11. Robert H. Jackson, *The Struggle for Judicial Supremacy: A Study of a Crisis in American Power Politics* (New York: Vintage Books, 1941), ix.

54. Jackson, "The Supreme Court," p. 12.

55. "Struggles over power that in Europe call out regiments of troops, in America call out battalions of lawyers. . . ." Jackson, *The Struggle for Judicial Supremacy,* p. xi.

56. Jackson, "The Supreme Court," p. 12.

57. For a striking example see *Everson* v. *Board of Education,* 330 U.S. 1 (1947), in Tussman, *The Supreme Court,* p. 211.

58. Felix Frankfurter, "The Process of Judging in the Supreme Court," in Westin, *The Supreme Court*, pp. 43–44.

59. Jackson, "The Supreme Court," p. 11.

60. McCloskey, *The American Supreme Court*, p. 7.

61. Owen J. Roberts, "Protecting the Court's Independence," in Westin, *The Supreme Court*, p. 100. For a thorough review of the issue see Leonard G. Ratner, "Congressional Power over the Appellate Jurisdiction of the Supreme Court," *University of Pennsylvania Law Review*, 109 (December 1960), 157–202.

62. Douglas, "In Defense of Dissent," p. 52.

63. See my reply to Emmons E. White in *The Christian Century*, 82 (March 10, 1965), 309.

64. Jackson, "The Supreme Court," p. 23.

65. *Ibid.*

66. Tussman, *The Supreme Court*, p. 142.

67. In a conference with a Jesuit in 1622, Bishop William Laud anchored "his whole system to the arbitrary word of God," while the Catholic argued "that if the authority of the Universal Church were disowned, the Bible would prove an inadequate substitute, because the Bible would become subject to individual interpretation, no two men would agree on what it meant, Protestantism would split into a hundred differing sects, each one twisting Biblical meanings to suit its own convenience, and thus scripture would lose all the necessary attributes of an authority." Miller and Johnson, *The Puritans*, pp. 41–42.

68. Jackson, "The Supreme Court," p. 66.

69. Westin, *The Supreme Court*, p. 37.

70. *Ibid.*

71. Jackson, "The Supreme Court," p. 82.

VII. RELIGION OF (OR AND) THE REPUBLIC

1. Keynote address of "A Symposium on Religion and the Republic," sponsored by the School of Religion of the University of Iowa, Iowa City, April 29–May 1, 1973.

2. I have long appreciated and used Stow Persons's suggestion that "A convincing demonstration of the pervasive effects of religion in its peculiar American forms will be made not by stressing formal religious history [i.e., "church" history] where secular historians talk about politics or

economics, but by showing how religious convictions have had their effects upon politics and economics . . . ;" Review of W. W. Sweet, *Religion in the Development of American Culture, 1765–1840*, in *William & Mary Quarterly*, IX (October 1952), 561.

3. This is in keeping with Henry May's claim that "the Recovery of American Religious History" provides, among other things, a direct way of studying the relation between ideas and institutions. *American Historical Review*, LXX (October 1964), 79–92.

4. See chapter II, above, "The Post-Protestant Concept and America's Two Religions," pp. 11–28.

5. See Winthrop S. Hudson, *Religion in America* (New York: Charles Scribner's Sons, 1965), p. 92: "The most noteworthy feature of this Deist 'creed' was its omissions. There was nothing distinctively Christian about it—no mention of any special work of Christ, of man's sinful nature and consequent need of redemption, or of any necessary dependence upon Biblical revelation. This was 'natural religion,' a term which points to the other source of Deism."

6. "Many Mansions," *American Historical Review*, XLIX (January 1964), 315. Of course, Brinton recognizes that ". . . certainly [this new religion was] related to, descended from, and by many reconciled with Christianity." A classical spelling-out of the continuity between medieval Christianity and the Enlightenment is Carl Becker's *The Heavenly City of Eighteenth Century Philosophers*.

7. It seemed strange to me that Novak entitled his article, "The Enlightenment Is Dead," and then devoted much of the content to argue the opposite, as suggested by the quotation above.

8. See chapter V, above, "Neither Church nor State," pp. 78–94.

9. John Herman Randall, Sr. and Jr., *Religion and the Modern World* (New York: Frederick A. Stokes Co., 1929), pp. 27–28. Still today, even among some otherwise "liberal" Christian leaders "accommodation" is a swear word.

10. The review, by Martin E. Marty, appeared in *The Christian Century*, October 11, 1972, 1021–22.

Index

SUBJECT INDEX